TEACHER'S GUIDE

YEARS 7 - 9

PART A

CONTENTS

INTRODUCTION

The Q Science Teacher's Guides have been written with the aim of providing easily accessible background information for each of the pupil's books.

For Years 7-9 (KS3) there are three Teacher's Guides, Parts A, B and C. Part A covers the individual explorations in Exploring Science Book 1, followed by the three Science Theme Books for Materials, then the two Science Theme books for Communications. Finally, the individual topics in The Nature of Science book are covered.

Throughout the pupil's books the numbered, blue symbols indicate possible pupil activities. These may be used in class, as homework or as assessment opportunities. Located throughout the books there are sections of work which have been printed on yellow backgrounds. These sections indicate areas or topics which pupils are likely to have met in the KS2 Programme of Study. They have been set in new contexts so that they can be used either as revision opportunities for the more able or as new learning opportunities for other pupils. Extension activities have been set in three-lined boxes.

EXPLORATION: How sharp is a drawing pin?

WAYS FORWARD

A discussion on what is meant by sharpness will indicate that there is no precise definition. A sharp knife will cut easily and a sharp drawing pin will be pushed into a piece of pinboard with relative ease.

Some pupils will compare the sharpness of different pins by seeing how easy it is to drive them a fixed distance into a surface, or by loading them with weights. Others will want to try to measure the area of the point of the pin; this could be attempted by using a microscope and a scale viewed together or, indirectly, by measuring the size of the hole created when the pin is pushed into a soft surface. Several dents side by side would be measured with less error than one dent alone.

Measuring apparatus like a micrometer can be used to give the diameter of the shank of the drawing pin. This will be larger than the pin end so will set an upper limit on the exploration measurement. This may provide an opportunity to consider a sharper and sharper pin. The limit of sharpness would be one molecule big.

MATERIALS, SAFETY, TIME

- Drawing pins (different varieties as available from most stationers).
- Transparent rulers.
- Microscopes and magnifying lenses.
- Surfaces to push pins into such as plasticine, wood, fibre board.
- For those who decide to compare the sharpness of different drawing pins, weights will be needed to apply similar forces.

Timing: 1 hour.

NATIONAL CURRICULUM ASSESSMENT OPPORTUNITIES

AT1	Level 5	SofA	b
AT8	Level 5	SofA	a
AT10	Level 5	SofA	c
	Level 6	SofA	b
AT17	Level 5	SofA	a

MY DESK

EXPLORATION: How well can a paper plane be made to fly?

WAYS FORWARD

To ensure that this exploration is more than a piece of very enjoyable fun, the principle of measuring the distance travelled by the paper plane must be clear to all pupils.

The exploration could be made to be motivating by having a competition whereby the plane that can fly a fixed distance, say five metres, with the least force would win. This would involve measuring the distance and the force.

If a fair test is to be made, the type of paper used and the area of paper used should be the same. A clue as to how the force imparted can be kept constant is shown in the pupil's book.

Pupils would benefit from considering where the energy stored in the moving plane eventually ends up. The idea that all energy changes lead to a warming of the environment, can be developed. The difficulty of then using this energy should be understood.

MATERIALS, SAFETY, TIME

- Paper, scissors, paper clips.
- Sticky tape and paper glue.
- Elastic bands.
- Rulers.

Timing: 1 hour.

NATIONAL CURRICULUM ASSESSMENT OPPORTUNITIES

AT1	Level 3	SofA	e,h
AT10	Level 4	SofA	a
	Level 6	SofA	a
AT13	Level 3	SofA	c
	Level 6	SofA	b

EXPLORATION: What can an eraser erase?

WAYS FORWARD

Can all erasers erase the same things? Do they erase as well? Is there a test for a good eraser? Can an eraser 'top ten' be produced? What happens when an eraser rubs out pencil lines?

Many other questions can be generated using a brainstorming exercise with a class. The ideas should be recorded so that they are visible to all the class; when the ideas appear to have ceased the more productive ones can be selected for further study.

Pupils need to be clear about what is to be tested. Many will need guidance so that they select a task which is achievable by them in the time available.

There are many variables to consider and changing just one of them at a time is difficult for many pupils. For example, if the ability of an eraser to rub out on different surfaces is chosen, then only the nature of the surface may be changed. The line drawn must be as similar as possible. Some pupils will realise that it is possible to compare the erasing properties by using different erasers on different portions of the same line. In fact, it would be possible to build a whole exploration around the need to draw a constant line on different surfaces.

Pupils will need to examine the line before and after the use of the eraser, probably with a microscope. The amount of damage to the surface, though difficult to quantify, would be a useful measure of the quality of an eraser.

MATERIALS, SAFETY, TIME

- Range of pencils from 3B to 2H.
- Pencil sharpener.
- Variety of colours of ink and ink pens. (It is best to use old-fashioned pens with only nibs, rather than have several fountain pens filled with different inks.)
- Paint (very difficult to remove from paper with an eraser).
- Access to different surfaces.
- Different types of paper, absorbent and shiny surfaces, glass, wood blocks.
- Variety of erasers, eg: the shaped ones on the top of pencils; rectangular blocks; quality erasers such as those supplied by Staedtler; typing rubbers and ink erasers.

Timing: 1 hour.

NATIONAL CURRICULUM ASSESSMENT OPPORTUNITIES

AT1	Level 4	SofA	i
AT6	Level 3	SofA	b
	Level 4	SofA	b

MY DESK

EXPLORATION: How many metres can a *Porter* write for?

WAYS FORWARD

The easiest *Porter* to test is a pencil, as the reduction in length of the lead is more rapid than for other writing implements. It is possible to weigh a pencil, use it and re-weigh it to gauge the life of the lead. A similar process can be used for an ink pen but the reduction in weight is less than for a pencil per metre of line drawn.

Other methods, such as measuring the length of a pencil lead, would work quite satisfactorily.

The amount of material used up in the *Porter* may well depend on the manner in which it is used, the type of paper which is used to write on, and other factors. The effects of these factors need to be taken into account. Two *Porters* could be compared, using a see-saw type balance to estimate if the various differences matter, before careful measurements are made.

It is important that the pencil or ink line is drawn with a uniform thickness and that a consistent pressure is applied. It will be easier to measure a long line, if the line follows a repetitive pattern whose distance can be measured. The total distance can then be calculated using a scaling factor.

MATERIALS, SAFETY, TIME

- Pencils (2HB are soft enough for rapid lead use), ink pens, biros, bottles of ink.
- Rulers.
- Paper of different surface textures.
- Sensitive balance.
- Straws and pins to make see-saw balance.

Timing: 1 hour.

NATIONAL CURRICULUM ASSESSMENT OPPORTUNITIES

AT10 Level 5 SofA c

EXPLORATION: How many different uses can you find for paper clips?

WAYS FORWARD

The properties of a paper clip need to be investigated and its uses tested. If pupils choose, for example, to investigate how good different paper clips are at being paper clips, then they will need to test such factors as how tightly the paper is gripped, and how well the paper clip recovers its shape after being used to hold several sheets of paper.

Other more divergent uses, such as to create a Braille alphabet, will also need to be tested to see if the idea is merely bizarre or novel and useful.

The use of paper clips in a number of different contexts could also be investigated, eg: as switches in electrical circuits; as magnets; as counterbalances in sensitive weighing machines; as fish hooks.

MATERIALS, SAFETY, TIME

- Paper clips in several sizes.
- Paper.
- Small weights and newton meters.
- Other items as decided by the nature of the use being investigated.

It would be useful for the provision of apparatus, if the planning was done at the end of one lesson and a list of requirements given ready for the next.

Timing: 1 hour for the exploration, plus 30 minutes for planning.

NATIONAL CURRICULUM ASSESSMENT OPPORTUNITIES

AT6   Level 7   SofA   b
AT10 Level 7   SofA   b

MY DESK

EXPLORATION: What surface does sticky tape stick to best?

WAYS FORWARD

A discussion would bring out the need to define what is meant by "stick to best". This could be quantified by the force needed to remove the tape, which could be small if it should be possible to remove without damage to the surface or large for uses such as sealing parcels. If the prime use is in order to attach something temporarily, then the lack of residue left by the tape would indicate the best surface.

The state of the surface might be significant and dampness affects the stickability of most glues. This can lead to an understanding that surface glues work by molecular attraction.

The method of measuring the force of adhesion of the tape to the surface, could be measured by hanging weights or pulling with a newton meter, although pupils, when allowed to make their own plans, will often arrive at solutions that are equally valid. Fair tests would ensure that the same area of tape was used, that the time to stick was the same for all tests and that the removal technique was constant.

MATERIALS, SAFETY, TIME

- Sticky tape, scissors, string.
- Small weight hooks and weights, newton meters.
- Variety of paper with different surfaces.
- Glass and plastic plates, wooden blocks.
- Steam generator.
- Metal plates.
- Magnifying apparatus to examine surface after tape has been removed.

Timing: 1 hour.

NATIONAL CURRICULUM ASSESSMENT OPPORTUNITIES

AT1	Level 4	SofA	c
AT6	Level 4	SofA	a
AT10	Level 4	SofA	d
	Level 5	SofA	c
	Level 7	SofA	a

EXPLORATION: Can painting a radiator make it give off more heat?

WAYS FORWARD

The difference between heat and temperature is important. More thermal energy, or heat, usually means a resulting rise in temperature but the value of this rise depends on the material and the mass being heated.

A model of a radiator could be a beaker or, more realistically, a metal can containing hot water. The surface could be altered by painting, adding corrugated paper (though the effect of the air trapped would be significant), or using cooking foil which can be rumpled or flat. A discussion of where the thermal energy goes from a can would show the need to account for the energy transferred through the base. This could be reduced with insulation or allowed by raising the can above the bench.

The way thermal energy is distributed may be investigated by placing thermometers around the radiator, including above it where convection will transfer warmed air. A thermometer inside the can would indicate its loss of thermal energy and that energy will have been transferred to the room. Pupils can be made aware that temperature measures the degree of hotness of an object.

Pupils should recognise that comparisons can only be made if the initial conditions are maintained. Two cans could be used, containing equal amounts of water at the same initial temperature. If the temperature changes, the effects of any differences may be seen. A wooden, insulated, lid should be used so that surface changes to the container dominate the thermal transfer process.

MATERIALS, SAFETY, TIME

- Beakers, metal cans (empty baked bean tins), hot water, thermometers, stop clocks.
- Various colours of rapid drying paint, cooking foil, coloured paper.
- Wooden lids, insulated stands, clamps to hold thermometers.

Thermometers are easily broken. If digital thermometers are not available, a sticky label attached to the thermometer can stop it rolling around.

Timing: I hour, plus homework for planning.

NATIONAL CURRICULUM ASSESSMENT OPPORTUNITIES

AT8	Level 6	SofA	b
AT9	Level 3	SofA	b
AT13	Level 4	SofA	d,e
	Level 7	SofA	a

HOME

EXPLORATION: What makes milk go stale?

WAYS FORWARD

Most pupils will be able to contribute to a discussion. They can be asked to describe the conditions when they have discovered stale milk. They will identify temperature, time, type of milk and can be guided towards impurities, and perhaps dirty containers, as important factors in accelerating the changes in milk. Other ideas should not be discouraged, as the identification of factors that do not accelerate the souring of milk are important. Refrigerators are dark inside, so is light a factor that contributes to milk souring? Does the presence of a small amount of sour milk accelerate the souring process?

Pupils should start with a hypothesis such as: "The higher the temperature, the faster milk goes off".

Different milk produces decay at different rates and under different conditions. These alternative milk products should be tested. Pupils should realise that a chemical change occurs as a material decays and a new material results.

Information can be obtained from the Milk Marketing Board (Thames Ditton, Surrey) and from many manufacturers of milk-related products. The effects that eating or drinking food that has deteriorated can have on humans, could be addressed here.

MATERIALS, SAFETY, TIME

• Milk: UHT, sterilised, pasteurised and powdered.
• Milk products such as butter, cheese and yoghurt, in small amounts,

Many pupils will identify the taste of sour milk but this could be an unsafe method of testing. Smell could be used but the increasing acidity would be more suitable. Resazurin dye changes colour and Methylene blue decolourises as a result of the bacterial enzymes which cause milk to go stale.

Timing: In many cases, souring will not occur within one day so the experiment will need to be checked at regular intervals over one week. To decide which areas to investigate needs one hour.

NATIONAL CURRICULUM ASSESSMENT OPPORTUNITIES

AT1	Level 3	SofA	a
AT2	Level 4	SofA	b
AT3	Level 5	SofA	d
AT6	Level 3	SofA	a
	Level 5	SofA	b
AT7	Level 4	SofA	a

EXPLORATION: How can you make old paper into something useful?

WAYS FORWARD

Pupils could be asked to list the different sources/types of paper products. The differences between these types could then be discussed, eg: colour, strength, thickness, printed or not, shape, surface finish. Different papers could be looked at under magnification and their surface and fibrous structure identified. What are the differences and what properties do these differences give to the paper product?

Different papers require different properties depending on their function and pupils should test each one accordingly, ie for: its wet and dry strengths, its store of thermal energy or insulating properties; its ability to absorb liquid; the amount of energy it releases when burnt.

Pupils may then decide to construct a useful item from some old paper. What they decide to make should have been guided by the testing completed earlier. Questions such as what is the best use for old newspaper have more than one correct answer!

MATERIALS, SAFETY, TIME

- Microscopes and magnifying glasses.
- A range of paper products: newspapers, writing paper, toilet tissue, kitchen roll, glossy magazines, recycled paper, paper bags, envelopes, greaseproof paper. These should be labelled.
- For strength testing: weights, hangers, sticky tape, string, balances, newton meters.
- For energy measurements: measuring cylinders, access to water, thermometers, clocks.
- Other equipment as identified by pupils according to their own requirements.

Timing: The work will need two sessions, one for the initial testing of waste paper and one for the production and consideration of the useful items created.

NATIONAL CURRICULUM ASSESSMENT OPPORTUNITIES

AT6	Level 4	SofA	a,b
	Level 6	SofA	a
	Level 7	SofA	a,b
AT10	Level 4	SofA	d
AT13	Level 7	SofA	a

HOME

EXPLORATION: How flat is flat?

WAYS FORWARD

Anything that can be flat in any sense of the word can be the focus for this exploration. Flatness should be discussed and a list of meanings created (a thesaurus would be useful). Groups can then discuss the area that they are interested in. These can be grouped into the following:

Mechanical flatness. This will require the measurement of small differences in height along a supposedly flat surface. This might involve a mapping of the profile of the surface, possible using feeler gauges.

Flatness in fizzy drink. This will require measuring the presence of any carbon dioxide still dissolved in the liquid. This can be encouraged to come out of solution by heating the liquid or possibly by adding sugar if the liquid is cola. The problem then becomes one of measuring the amount of gas. This may involve simply collecting the gas in a plastic bag and getting an approximate volume measurement, or a more detailed study as in the exploration *How much air can a balloon hold?* (Pupil's book page 45).

Flat batteries. The measurement will require electrical circuits that detect a small current, such as a sensitive ammeter connected across the battery with a 1000 ohm resistor connected in parallel as a safety device. The apparatus used in this exploration must be treated with great care.

Flat music. This can be explored using an oscilloscope and a microphone to display the trace. This can be compared to the quantified trace from a calibrated signal generator or from a tuning fork or other musical instrument. Some musical aptitude, would be useful for this exploration!

MATERIALS, SAFETY, TIME

- Mechanical flatness: rulers, magnifying glasses, feeler gauges, techniques for measuring the thickness of one sheet of paper by measuring 100 (could be available on a worksheet). A nominally flat surface such as a metal block or strip.
- Flat drinks: see page 45, relating to *How much air can a balloon hold?*
- Flat batteries: flat cells of any sort, but note that car batteries or other rechargeable cells may give very large currents. It is unwise to allow pupils unsupervised access to such batteries. Resistors of several hundred ohms, ammeters and voltmeters in micro and milli ranges, light beam galvanometer, wires, crocodile clips, bulbs, motors, clock.
- Flat music: oscilloscope, signal generator, tuning forks, stringed instruments.

Timing: depends on the activity chosen.

NATIONAL CURRICULUM ASSESSMENT OPPORTUNITIES

Many opportunities, depending on the activity chosen.

EXPLORATION: How can I make a bath *full* alarm?

WAYS FORWARD

To detect the level of water in a bath, a change needs to occur. This could be a change in water mass or volume in the bath, a change in the water tank, or perhaps a measurement of the water volume into the tank by measuring the flow through the taps. Two methods are likely to predominate: the idea of a float, such as the duck in the picture, or the conduction of water between two contacts to complete a circuit. Tap water will conduct reasonably at low voltages but added bath salts can make water conduct well. Other additives could be tried.

The differing levels for different users can be obtained by having a device which is adjusted for each user. Pupils who have some experience with computers may be able to devise such a solution and the computer could be programmed to give the alarm at the required level.

The picture shows a girl with headphones and observant pupils will realise that the alarm needs to have an optical output to attract her attention.

Pupils with access to more sophisticated construction apparatus may consider the possibility of turning the taps on and off automatically.

MATERIALS, SAFETY, TIME

- Computer or Vela, apparatus for simple circuit, wires, metal plates about 10cm, waterproof tape, plasticine, ruler, bath salts, beakers and bulbs.

- Mains electricity is not allowed in bathrooms!!

NATIONAL CURRICULUM ASSESSMENT OPPORTUNITIES

AT1	Level 4	SofA	g
AT11	Level 3	SofA	a,b
	Level 4	SofA	a
	Level 5	SofA	b
AT12	Level 4	SofA	a
	Level 7	SofA	c

HOME

EXPLORATION: Just how strong *is* wallpaper paste?

WAYS FORWARD

There are several variables that need to be identified so that they can be controlled and not varied inadvertently. The factors which might matter are: time; temperature; type of paper (wallpaper is not suitable as it comes away from its backing paper); mix of paste; type of surface; rate of setting. Pupils may decide that there are others, if encouraged to discuss in groups.

Measuring paste strength can be achieved by pulling a pasted section apart with weights. Probably, pupils will decide to use different versions of this technique.

Results could be organised in tabular form or bar graphs to enable different groups to compare results from different experiments.

While the paste is drying, pupils could have the drying process explained. The liquid evaporates and chemical bonds are formed.

MATERIALS, SAFETY, TIME

- Wallpaper paste or a mix of flour and water can be used.
- Weights and hangers, newton meters.
- Different types if paper, different surfaces such as wood, brick, breeze block, cardboard.
- Hairdryer to heat up paste, steam generator.

Timing: Time needed depends on the time for the paste to set. This is likely to be more than one hour so samples should be set up during one lesson for testing in the next.

NATIONAL CURRICULUM ASSESSMENT OPPORTUNITIES

AT1	Level 4	SofA	h
AT6	Level 4	SofA	a,b
AT8	Level 4	SofA	a
AT10	Level 5	SofA	b

EXPLORATION: Which stomach powder is the best?

WAYS FORWARD

After initial class discussion of the different types of stomach powders available, their medical use and the cost of them, pupils could discuss in groups what "best" could mean in this case, eg:
a) the cheapest
b) needing the smallest amount in order to neutralise acid
c) the most attractive
d) the fastest-acting

Some pupils may need help in realising that the powders/tablets may need weighing out in order to have a fair test, as two different tablets are not necessarily the same mass.

To find out the amount required to neutralise acid:

mass of powder at start   =   g
mass of powder left at end =   g
mass of powder used   =   g

Relate the cost to the amount needed.

As an extension, pupils could write word equations for the reaction, finding out from the packets what is the main constituent in the tablet. They could also work out the products of the reactions (a salt).

MATERIALS, SAFETY, TIME

- Balance, small spoons or spatulas, dilute hydrochloric acid.
- Different types of antacids.
- Beakers, universal indicator solution, measuring cylinders.

Timing: 30 minutes

NATIONAL CURRICULUM ASSESSMENT OPPORTUNITIES

AT 6   Level 5   SofA   b
      Level 9   SofA   b

YOU AND YOUR BODY

EXPLORATION: What is your reaction time?

WAYS FORWARD

Discuss why we need fast reaction times. Pupils may also need help in realising that speed is related to distance and time, ie:

$$\text{speed} = \frac{\text{distance travelled (M)}}{\text{time taken (S)}}$$

Qualitative assessments of speed can be looked at, within the same type of experiment.

The experiments could be performed at different times of the day, eg before and after lunch to show the effect of having a meal. To save some time, different groups could look at different experiments and the results could be drawn together at the end.

Consider the different factors which can make reaction rates slow down. Age could be investigated although alcohol cannot.

MATERIALS, SAFETY, TIME

- Tubing (opaque) with small balls (possibly marbles) which will pass through the tubing.
- Metre rulers.
- Stop clocks.
- Snap cards, or other equipment according to pupils' requirements.

Timing: 1 hour.

NATIONAL CURRICULUM ASSESSMENT OPPORTUNITIES

AT3   Level 4   SofA   b
AT10 Level 6   SofA   a

YOU AND YOUR BODY

EXPLORATION: **Prepare a talk or booklet to tell a younger person how to keep healthy.**

WAYS FORWARD

This exploration would be best approached in groups of 2-3 pupils. It involves a literature search, both of pamphlets from the Health Education Council and of the library or science department library. The emphasis should be on resource-based learning.

The language the pupils use in their booklets should be simple enough for a young person to read, with lots of pictures or diagrams. This will prevent copying directly from other books.

The teacher must be released to go around to the different groups and ask questions about what the groups have learnt. The exploration should also be drawn together at the end either by pupils giving talks or by the teacher doing so.

The work should be displayed afterwards for all to see.

As an extension, pupils could research, and then give an account of, an advance in medicine - naming the scientist and the life and times in which the scientist worked.

MATERIALS, SAFETY, TIME

- Materials for preparing a booklet: paper, scissors, pencils, felt-tips, etc.
- Booklets from the Health Education Council on healthy eating, smoking, alcohol, teeth and gums, exercise, etc. You can get these from your local Health Education Centre or clinic free of charge.
- Poster paper and OHP sheets and pens for those wishing to do talks.

Timing: 1 week.

NATIONAL CURRICULUM ASSESSMENT OPPORTUNITIES

AT3   Level 4   SofA   b
         Level 5   SofA   b
AT17   Level 4   SofA   a

YOU AND YOUR BODY

EXPLORATION: How sensitive is your hand?

WAYS FORWARD

Discuss how we feel things, which parts of our bodies are sensitive, and which are not. Introduce the idea of nerve cells and what they do. The idea that there are many different types of cells in the body which have different functions can be introduced here. Pupils may think about the use of the hands to read, with the Braille alphabet.

The exploration is fairly simple. Obviously the person being tested (it is suggested the pupils work in pairs) should be blindfolded so they cannot see the stimuli.

The exact temperature of the surroundings should be measured, ie the temperature of cold water and hot water, so that a worthwhile comparison between temperature and sensitivity can be measured.

Do all people have the same sensitivity in their hands? Are different parts of the hand more sensitive than others? This could be investigated by touching the skin with either 1 pin or 2 pins close together. The subject has to decide whether 0, 1 or 2 pins were felt. Repetition of this will give a percentage success rate for different parts of the hand.

MATERIALS, SAFETY, TIME

- Blindfolds.
- Sharp instruments, eg pencils.
- Blunt instruments, eg rulers.
- Feathers, ice cubes.
- Bowl, access to warm water, thermometers.

Timing: 1 hour.

NATIONAL CURRICULUM ASSESSMENT OPPORTUNITIES

AT3   Level 5   SofA   a
AT13 Level 3   SofA   b

YOU AND YOUR BODY

EXPLORATION: Make a labelled model or picture to show the main parts of the human body.

WAYS FORWARD

Pupils may draw their own picture, make a model, or use photocopied sheets of the parts, cutting them out and sticking them together.

After they have done this, they could investigate the names of the organs and their functions. If the sheet is large enough, they may be encouraged to label their diagrams; if they have made models, this could be done as a separate table.

Classify the parts into different systems, eg: CNS, Digestive, Skeletal.

MATERIALS, SAFETY, TIME

- Photocopied sheets of the parts of the body, which could be cut out. These could be enlarged to A3 size.
- Glue.
- The teacher could use a large model or poster for display at the end.

Timing: 1-2 hours.

NATIONAL CURRICULUM ASSESSMENT OPPORTUNITIES

AT3   Level 4   SofA   a
       Level 5   SofA   e

YOU AND YOUR BODY

EXPLORATION: How often does the heart beat?

WAYS FORWARD

Small group discussion should include:
- Why the heart beats.
- How the heart beat can be measured - finding pulse spots.
- Does the heart beat always stay the same?

Pupils should be encouraged to look at the effects of different conditions on the heart beat. The following should be included:
- After a meal.
- Being relaxed, eg after listening to soothing music.
- After exercise. (A graph of the length of exercise, in minutes, vs pulse rate is a possible method of recording.)
- A bar chart or tables could be used to record the overall findings.

As an extension, consider whether all people have the same pulse rate before or after exercise. The heart beat rate in relation to the respiration rate can also be considered.

MATERIALS, SAFETY, TIME

- Stop clocks.

Timing: 1 hour

NATIONAL CURRICULUM ASSESSMENT OPPORTUNITIES

AT1   Level 3   SofA   d,f
        Level 6   SofA   a(iv)
AT3   Level 5   SofA   e

EXPLORATION: Make pure water conduct electricity in as many ways as you can.

WAYS FORWARD

Pupils will need to recognise that a series circuit will allow testing of conduction. They should test distilled water initially to confirm that it does not conduct but will need to test that their circuit does work, perhaps by shorting out the water section.

A variety of materials should be available, those which dissolve and those which do not, to allow a possible pattern to be developed. The first requirement is that the substance added should dissolve. However, all soluble substances do not then allow conduction. What has to happen is that the substance dissociates into ions, charged parts, which can then carry the current in the liquid. The idea that the current in a liquid is due to charges that are free to move, may be developed for some pupils.

Quantitative measurements are possible, especially if pupils are ready to use ammeters. The brightness of a bulb will give some indication of current flow.

Able pupils could set up several circuits or several parallel branches, to allow the simultaneous testing and better comparison of different materials. Pupils may notice electrolysis effects but this is a difficult area. The precise effects depend on the electrode and the nature of the electrolyte. To have the chance of any observable effects, the power supply should be capable of driving at least one ampere, so a power pack is better than dry cells.

When a current flows other things happen, such as gas release, thermal energy evolved, material deposited on the electrodes dipping into the liquid. As an extension, pupils could observe these effects and perhaps try to explain what might be happening.

MATERIALS, SAFETY, TIME

- DC transformer up to 6V, connecting wires, crocodile clips, beakers, distilled water.

- Materials to try could include: common salt, chalk dust, copper sulphate (with a safety warning), potassium permanganate, zinc granules, bubble bath, bath salts, vinegar, dilute sulphuric acid, copper turnings, tap water.

- To act as electrodes, the following can be tried: copper foil, carbon rods, crocodile clips themselves and zinc plates.

Timing: 1 hour.

NATIONAL CURRICULUM ASSESSMENT OPPORTUNITIES

AT1	Level 4	SofA	j
AT7	Level 6	SofA	b
AT11	Level 3	SofA	a,b
	Level 4	SofA	a
	Level 5	SofA	b
	Level 7	SofA	b

ELECTRICKERY

EXPLORATION: Find as many ways as you can of showing that an electric current is in a wire.

WAYS FORWARD

Electricity flows and several different effects result. The effects are heating, magnetic fields and chemical effects. This exploration will provide the opportunity for pupils to note these effects. It is up to the teacher to persuade pupils to elaborate on their observation. For example, a pupil who says the light bulb glows should be asked why. If the idea is put forward of something moving in the wire, heating the wire by friction and this heating causing the wire filament to glow, then this pupil could be said to have developed a good concept of electricity.

Pupils should be encouraged to investigate an effect fully. For example, a pupil who places a compass near a wire, switches on the current and notices the compass needle changing direction, should go on to investigate the shape of that field. Investigate what happens if the current is switched off, how far from the wire the magnetic effect can be detected and what shape the field is.

For the chemical effect by choosing carbon rods and copper sulphate solution, the mass/current/time effects can be investigated.

MATERIALS, SAFETY, TIME

- Power packs, connecting wire, bulbs, magnets, plotting compasses, copper plates, copper sulphate solution, carbon rods, ammeters and voltmeters, coils of nichrome wire for heaters, iron filings, balance to mass to 1/10 gm.

- The only safety problem is that large currents of the order of four amperes are needed to have significant measurable magnetic fields. These currents heat up connecting wires.

Timing: 1 hour per effect.

NATIONAL CURRICULUM ASSESSMENT OPPORTUNITIES

AT1	Level 5	SofA	c
AT11	Level 5	SofA	b,c
	Level 6	SofA	a,c
	Level 7	SofA	a,b

EXPLORATION: How much light do you need to see to read?

WAYS FORWARD

The measurement of amount of light is difficult. It could be put in the context of interior design in terms of deciding how subdued the lighting in a home could be while still allowing the occupants to read the TV guides. The amount of light could be measured using a photographic light meter or more simply an ORP light dependent resistor connected in a circuit to indicate the variation of resistance with light falling. Or pupils might simply use the current flowing in a circuit with a bulb to indicate the light energy emitted.

Pupils who wear spectacles could be tested with and without them.

The inverse square law may be used to vary the light intensity. If a small light source is used, then moving it twice as far away will reduce the light intensity by four times. Three times as far away gives a nine times reduction. The eye does not respond linearly, ie we do not perceive a reduction of four times for a doubling of distance. In fact, the actual level has to fall by one hundred times before we perceive a halving of the light intensity.

Clearly, the colour of light matters and this should form part of the whole exploration.

Sight defects such as short sight, long sight, colour blindness and astigmatism can be introduced here. This could be put forward as a reason for getting different results from different subjects.

MATERIALS, SAFETY, TIME

- Variety of light sources.
- Cardboard boxes to make light tight viewing spaces.
- ORP cells connected to 1.5 volt cell and ammeter.
- Photographic light meter.
- Rulers.
- Copies of grey/black page of text.

Timing: 1 hour.

NATIONAL CURRICULUM ASSESSMENT OPPORTUNITIES

AT11	Level 4	SofA	a
	Level 5	SofA	b
AT12	Level 4	SofA	b
AT15	Level 4	SofA	a
	Level 6	SofA	b,c

ELECTRICKERY

EXPLORATION: How much electricity is used in your home?

WAYS FORWARD

Most electrical appliances in the home use mains, 240V, electricity. The energy supplied is metered and charged for in units. One unit of electricity would be used by a one kilowatt device on for one hour. Pupils should be able to calculate the number of units of electricity a device will use, provided they know the number of watts and the time the appliance is used for . One bar of an electric fire is likely to be a one kilowatt device. Pupils should realise the types of devices that are high power, generally those with any heating element such as a kettle, fire or cooker and those that are low power, such as lighting or sound.

Pupils should be shown how to read an electricity bill, including details such as the standing charge indicated.

The simplest way forward would be to ask pupils to read their electricity meter over a period of time and record the readings. For a better understanding of the costs involved in electrical energy, pupils could record the meter reading with different devices switched on and compare the recorded use from the meter with the stated power of the device. The energy/power used can start a discussion of the need for efficient devices that use as little energy as possible, as a matter of conservation and economy.

An approach which allows a range of abilities to succeed is to ask pupils to draw a simple plan of their home and to add the electrical information. This would be for homework.

MATERIALS, SAFETY, TIME

- This is most likely to be an exploration where the results are taken at home. Some pupils would find this difficult to arrange, so a duplicated set of real results should be made available.

- Examples of electricity bills and photographs of the real device showing the power consumption.

- Any work with mains electricity has potential dangers and pupils should only investigate with the agreement of a responsible adult.

Timing: 1 hour plus 2 homeworks, preferably separated by a few days.

NATIONAL CURRICULUM ASSESSMENT OPPORTUNITIES

AT1	Level 3	SofA	b
AT11	Level 6	SofA	d
AT13	Level 5	SofA	a

EXPLORATION: What makes a good fuse?

WAYS FORWARD

The purpose of a fuse, to melt when the current is too large, needs to be made apparent. Pupils need a circuit in which there is the possibility of varying and measuring the current.

Pupils might choose to investigate what materials could be used as a fuse, although this would be difficult. Alternatively, they could investigate whether two pieces of, say, one ampere fuse wire wrapped together make a two ampere fuse (they should find that they will, if the wires are in parallel and each part is carrying one ampere). They could see that the length does not matter unless it is very small and the connections dissipate a lot of heat.

The effect of coiling the fuse wire, without shorting it, could be tried by wrapping it around a thin dowel. A closely coiled wire would melt at a lower current as it is less easy to dissipate the heat generated. Faster groups might like to see the effect of cooling the fuse with an air flow, or perhaps ice. Would a fuse work the same way for an Eskimo in an igloo? There is no electricity in an igloo! The temperature at which fuse wire melts could be found by using a suitable thermometer. It would need to read to 500°.

The convenience of cartridge fuses over fuse wire should be explained, although fuse wire is a much more convenient package for this investigation.

The purpose of a fuse is to protect the device it is connected to. If a fault develops and a large current flows, then the fuse will melt and disconnect the device from the electricity supply. It does not itself protect the user. A current sufficient to give a person an electric shock can flow yet not blow the fuse.

The reason for an earth connection is likely to be requested by aware pupils. This protects the user if the case of the electrical device becomes live. A large current flows and the fuse melts, cutting off the electricity supply.

MATERIALS, SAFETY, TIME

- Fuse wire (one amp and five amp).
- Power supply capable of delivering a few amperes (not dry cells).
- Crocodile clips or better screw terminals.
- Ammeter if measurements are to be made.
- Bulbs (24/36 watt for car headlamp is suitable), hair dryer or fan.
- Access to ice, thermometer to 500°, dowels of range of diameters to 10mm, rulers, magnifying glass to investigate molten ends of wire.

Timing: 1 hour.

NATIONAL CURRICULUM ASSESSMENT OPPORTUNITIES

AT1	Level 4	SofA	f
AT11	Level 4	SofA	a
	Level 5	SofA	b

ELECTRICKERY

EXPLORATION: What affects how well a rubbed balloon sticks to a surface?

WAYS FORWARD

Electrostatic explorations are very difficult but this one has the advantage that there is no correct answer! It could be introduced with a demonstration of a rubbed balloon being stuck to a wall. The class can be asked to predict how long the balloon will stay attached. In one test, the author has managed to find a balloon stuck to a wall for more than 24 hours!

Pupils can investigate the effects of: rubbing with different materials; trying different surfaces to attach the balloon to; different amounts of rubbing (is one rub as good as several?); the state of the surface, ie wet, hot or cold.

For more adventurous pupils, the force needed to remove a balloon from the wall can be measured. Does it change with time? Are all balloons equally well stuck?

General problems associated in the real world with a build-up of electrostatic charge can be discussed within the context of this exploration.

MATERIALS, SAFETY, TIME

- Plenty of different shaped balloons.
- Variety of material to rub against balloons, eg: wool, cotton, silk, glass, wood, nylon, plastic. The materials should be labelled.
- Clocks with a possibility of timing several hours.
- Small weights, string, cotton, small value newton meters, balance to measure to 1/10 gm.

Timing: 1 hour for the practical work, but the observations could take another 24 hours.

NATIONAL CURRICULUM ASSESSMENT OPPORTUNITIES

AT10 Level 4   SofA   d
AT11 Level 6   SofA   c
      Level 7   SofA   c

THE PICNIC

EXPLORATION: Which would be the best type of nuts to take on a picnic?

WAYS FORWARD

The energy stored in nuts is chemical energy. Discuss how it can be released and then measured. The nuts can be burnt and the heat used to increase the temperature of water.

To construct fair tests, pupils may need help in realising that the mass of the nuts and the amount of water must be the same. If the mass of the nuts is not the same, they will need help in working out the temperature rise of the water if 1g of nut was used. The mass of the nuts left at the end will need to be measured to do this.

Extension: Energy = mass x specified heat x temperature rise
             of water capacity of
             used   water
       (J)   (g)   (4.18)   (°C)

The Joule could be introduced, without derivation, as a measurement of energy.

Relate the relative values of nuts to the energy values on the packets. How do they compare?

As the mass of H_2O and the specific heat capacity remain constant in experiments, the energy is proportional to the temperature rise. Pupils should be aware that the greater the temperature rise of the water, the more energy the nuts contain.

This experiment provides further practice in the use of the balance and the thermometer.

MATERIALS, SAFETY, TIME

- Many different types of nuts, shelled and unshelled, eg: peanuts, walnuts, hazelnuts, brazil nuts, almonds, pecans.
- Mounted needles, corks.
- Retort stand and clamps.
- Foil to act as a heat shield.

Timing: 1-2 hours.

NATIONAL CURRICULUM ASSESSMENT OPPORTUNITIES

AT13 Level 4   SofA b,d

THE PICNIC

EXPLORATION: How can the browning of sliced apple be stopped?

WAYS FORWARD

This is a very easy experiment to perform for pupils of all abilities. They could discuss ideas in small groups initially.

There is a difference between 'slowing down' and 'stopping' browning!

Enzymic browning can be investigated by heating the apple slices, eg by placing them in boiling water.

By preventing the apple from coming into contact with the air, is browning stopped or slowed down, ie is there an element of oxidation by air?

The experiment could lead on to a discussion relating methods of slowing down apple browning and methods of industrial food preservation, ie, canning in syrup, adding lemon juice to fruit salads.

MATERIALS, SAFETY, TIME

- Apples, cooking and eating.
- Knives, tiles for cutting on.
- Cling film, vinegar, lemons, salt, sugar, flour.
- Stop clocks.
- Bunsen burners (optional).

- Care must be taken with sharp knives.

Timing: 1 hour.

NATIONAL CURRICULUM ASSESSMENT OPPORTUNITIES

AT7   Level 7   SofA b

EXPLORATION: How much is there in a can of cola?

WAYS FORWARD

A whole can of cola per pupil or group is unnecessary. Rather, give them a test tube or boiling tube with 10-40cm. Pupils may need help in realising that a can of cola contains a liquid *and* a gas. The amount of liquid and gas can be measured by a)volume or b)mass.

Pupils wishing to follow either line will need to extract the gas (bubbles) from the liquid. This could be done by adding (a known mass) sugar.

a) The gas is collected by suitable means and the volume measured.

b) mass of closed can + liquid + gas =
   mass of can =
   mass of liquid + gas =
   mass of gas =

What is the gas?

MATERIALS, SAFETY, TIME

- 4 cans or 1 large bottle of cola.
- Test tubes or boiling tube.
- Sugar lumps.
- Measuring cylinders.
- Balance.

Timing: 1 hour

NATIONAL CURRICULUM ASSESSMENT OPPORTUNITIES

AT1	Level 4	SofA	a,b,d,e,i
	Level 5	SofA	a,c
AT6	Level 4	SofA	c,e

THE PICNIC

EXPLORATION: How would *you* test the packaging?

WAYS FORWARD

Pupils need to think about the simple properties the packaging needs to have, but the emphasis in this exploration should be on the testing of materials.

The relationship between the properties of the materials and their everyday uses should be considered.

Pupils can test whether the material is biodegradable by burying it, although a longer time will be required for the results of this test.

The actual methods of testing will vary from group to group. Wherever they can, they should be encouraged to make their test quantitative.

As an extension, pupils could find out the cost of the materials and hence evaluate the choice of material, strength and cost.

MATERIALS, SAFETY, TIME

- Any packaging materials, eg: crisp packets, biscuit wrappers, fruit juice cartons, carrier bags, paper bags, cans, etc.
- Child proof containers.
- Weights for measuring strength.
- Clamps and stands.
- Ink block and stamp.

Timing: 1 hour.

NATIONAL CURRICULUM ASSESSMENT OPPORTUNITIES

AT6	Level 4	SofA a,b
AT10	Level 5	SofA c
	Level 7	SofA b

THE PICNIC

EXPLORATION: What makes the best food (or drink) container for a picnic?

WAYS FORWARD

This exploration could be approached by explaining that the groups within the class are research and development teams from a company. Each group should discuss what 'best' means with respect to a food/drink container for a picnic. Does it keep the food hot/cold? Does it stop the food being squashed/broken, etc? They must then decide which food/drink they want to use. A hot drink can easily be substituted by hot water.

The pupils should be given time to test the material for simple properties, eg strength, hardness, flexibility, solubility, etc. They should be allowed to test these in their own way, although they may need help.

To bring the investigation to a conclusion, a container report could be submitted by the different groups, either written or as a verbal presentation. The presentation should include sections on:
- The type of food container needed.
- The container which best fits the job.
- The type of material used.
- Why?

MATERIALS, SAFETY, TIME

- Vacuum flask.
- Glass and plastic bottles.
- Polystyrene disposable cups and lids.
- Crisps and crisp packets.
- Boiled eggs (or plasticine as a substitute) and sandwiches.
- Boxes as substitute for a hamper basket.
- Thermometers.
- Bunsen burners.
- Weights.

Timing: 1-2 hours.

NATIONAL CURRICULUM ASSESSMENT OPPORTUNITIES

AT6 Level 4   SofA a,b
     Level 7   SofA a,b

EXPLORING SCIENCE

THE PICNIC

EXPLORATION: How quickly does food go off?

WAYS FORWARD

How can the pupils tell if food has gone off? What would they see? These points could be discussed in small groups.

If the pupils are testing whether all foods go off at the same rate, then the conditions must remain constant whilst the types of food change.

If the pupils are testing how different conditions affect the food, then the food should remain the same (eg bread) but the conditions should change, ie temperature, moisture, compressed or not, open/closed containers.

The speed of decay could be measured by placing a polythene bag with a grid drawn on it, around the food. Pupils should then check at daily intervals to see how much of the food is covered with fungi.

MATERIALS, SAFETY, TIME

- Bread, cheese, fruit etc. Any types of picnic foods.
- Access to a fridge or cool box (with ice packs).

- Food must not be eaten in a laboratory.
- Do not grow any anaerobic bacteria.
- Avoid breathing in the spores of fungi.
- Do not touch bacterial colonies.

Timing: 1 week.

NATIONAL CURRICULUM ASSESSMENT OPPORTUNITIES

AT2   Level 4   SofA   b
AT7   Level 7   SofA   b

EXPLORATION: How should a car ferry be loaded?

WAYS FORWARD

Pupils could be asked about their journeys on the sea. Many will have travelled abroad or to the islands around Britain.

The main element of this work is the balance of a car ferry. Clearly the safety aspect of this in real life is paramount. Many pupils will have developed the idea that a system is unstable if heavy loads are put high up. A simple demonstration using a bunsen burner, or similar, can show how unstable an object can be by trying to balance the bunsen burner upside down. Imbalance will result in turning forces which could topple the ferry. The amount of imbalance depends on the weight of the load and the distance from the lengthwise axis of the ferry.

This exploration gives a chance to progress with this idea. A discussion would clarify how well developed pupils' ideas already are on this matter.

It may be better for pupils not to float their model ferry but to load it and tilt it to see how stable it is.

Pupils may like to write to car ferry companies to gain information. Some useful addresses are:

Brittany Ferries   P&O European Ferries
Mill Bay Docks   Channel House
Plymouth   Channel View Road
PL1 3EW   Dover
                       Kent   CT17 9TJ

MATERIALS, SAFETY, TIME

- Wood to model the ferry, which could be simply a flat-bottomed raft.
- Cardboard to allow a deck structure to be made.
- Some toy cars and lorries, or wooden blocks to represent these.
- Protractors, plumb line.

Timing: From 1 hour up to a major project.

NATIONAL CURRICULUM ASSESSMENT OPPORTUNITIES

AT10 Level 6   SofA c
      Level 8   SofA a

HOLIDAYS

EXPLORATION: Design a set of devices to measure and record the weather.

WAYS FORWARD

Discuss what is meant by the weather, to bring out the easily measurable aspects such as temperature, rainfall, wind speed and direction, air pressure, hours of sunlight, humidity. The effects of climate on agriculture can create a reason for such measurements needing to be completed.

The opportunity should be taken to explain that wind is air in motion. This will serve to reinforce the idea that air exists in a layer about 40 km thick, which covers the surface of the Earth.

There are obvious areas where the recording power of a computer would be useful. A thermocouple connected to a computer would enable measurements to be taken over an extended period of time.

Methods of recording and displaying the results should be discussed and the idea of a symbolic representation should occur to some pupils. Examples could be provided from the newspaper or from the television weather reports.

Groups of pupils could work on different aspects of the weather recording, with their work brought together to form a class project. Pupils could extend the work to provide a regular weather report for the whole school.

MATERIALS, SAFETY, TIME

- Thermometer, clock, aneroid barometer.
- Card or cloth to construct a wind sock.
- Wood and other materials to construct an anemometer to measure wind speed (a windmill pulling up a measured length of string and a stop clock will do quite well).
- Dynamo.
- Example of weather map.
- Access to computer monitoring equipment.

Timing: From 1 hour up to a major project.

NATIONAL CURRICULUM ASSESSMENT OPPORTUNITIES

AT1	Level 3	SofA	d,g
AT9	Level 3	SofA	e
	Level 4	SofA	a,b

EXPLORATION: What's the best ice to use?

WAYS FORWARD

Discussion about how to make ice lumps, can indicate the fact that ice can be colder than 0°C.

The different ways of measuring amount need to be made clear. Does the volume or mass matter? If mass is chosen to be the factor varied, then the conservation of mass on a change of state can be involved. Devising fair tests is important here.

The size of the ice lump compared to the size of the glass is an important design consideration.

Ice lumps for cooling drinks do not have to be made from ice, nor do they have to melt into the drink. Ideas such as cooling the drink from outside the glass should be allowed. The drop in temperature must be measured for different cooling devices but clearly the same amount of drink must be used and the container must be constant, to allow a fair test.

Possible extensions are: to survey and find out what temperature is preferable for cool drinks; to investigate the effect of altering the surface area by crushing the ice; to attempt to produce reusable ice cubes (try freezing water in a plastic freezer bag).

MATERIALS, SAFETY, TIME

- Water, plastic bags, thermometers, stirrers, beakers.
- Volume measurement and weighing apparatus.
- Supply of ice.
- Hammer and cloth to crush ice.
- Safety glasses.

Timing: 1 hour.

NATIONAL CURRICULUM ASSESSMENT OPPORTUNITIES

AT1	Level 3	SofA	c
AT6	Level 4	SofA	d
AT8	Level 4	SofA	a
	Level 6	SofA	b
AT13	Level 4	SofA	c,d,e

HOLIDAYS

EXPLORATION: How does the shadow change with the lighting?

WAYS FORWARD

Introduce this exploration by discussing shadows and where they are formed. A working description of a shadow is "the region where no light goes". By the end of the exploration, pupils can be expected to realise that shadows can contain structure and that umbra is where no light goes but penumbra is a gradual gradation of less light.

The fact that the size of the shadow depends on the positioning of the light source is within the grasp of most pupils. However, the fact that it is the ratio, ie

$$\frac{\text{distance from object to screen}}{\text{distance from source to object}}$$

that gives magnification, is a difficult idea which can only be shown with careful measurement.

A small-sized light source will give a clear, sharp-edged shadow with little penumbra, while an extended source such as a table lamp will give a blurred shadow because of the less dark shadow around the edge.

A regular shape is better for size measurements, but a person shape is more fun.

The shape of shadows is most easily explained if we say that light travels in straight lines. The phenomenon is known as rectilinear propagation.

With two large light sources and coloured filters, it is possible to introduce the idea of colour mixing, by shining different coloured lights together to cast coloured shadows. The effect is also very pretty.

Some word definitions:
umbra - the dark part of a shadow in the centre.
penumbra - the fuzzy part of the shadow at the edges. Not as dark as the umbra.
rectilinear propagation - rectilinear means straight lines and propagation simply means travel.

MATERIALS, SAFETY, TIME

- Table lamp or angle poise.
- Small bright bulb (compact light source).
- Rulers, card and graph paper for accurate size determination.
- Clamp to hold card shape.
- Coloured filters.

Timing: 30 minutes.

NATIONAL CURRICULUM ASSESSMENT OPPORTUNITIES

AT1	Level 4	SofA	d
AT15	Level 4	SofA	b

EXPLORATION: What is the best shape for the sail on a windsurfer?

WAYS FORWARD

At the simplest level, a sail is meant to push the windsurfer along. The force created by a wind on different types of sail can be measured and compared.

An alternative that may will occur to pupils is to find the sail which gives the windsurfer maximum speed.

Force may be measured directly with a newton meter or indirectly by measuring acceleration.

At a higher level, the effect of changing the angle of the sail to the wind may be investigated and even the ability of the sail to act as an aerofoil and propel the windsurfer at an acute angle into the wind.

A variety of materials for the sail may be tried.

If a long water tank is required, the covers on some flourescent lights may be used. These provide a rectangular cross-section tank about 1.5 metres long which can have the ends sealed.

MATERIALS, SAFETY, TIME

- Pieces of wood for the sailboard, dowel for the mask, means of shaping wood, glue.
- Newton metres to 10N max.
- Water tank.
- Elastic bands, variety of possible sail materials, scissors.
- Timing devices, rulers.

Timing: 1 - 2 hours.

NATIONAL CURRICULUM ASSESSMENT OPPORTUNITIES

AT1   Level 5   SofA a
AT10   Level 5   SofA a,c,d
       Level 6   SofA a,b

HOLIDAYS

EXPLORATION: Design and test a waterproof camera case.

WAYS FORWARD

The difficulties which one would expect to encounter are with the waterproofing ability and with the amount of distortion of the light when passing through the materials of the transparent, waterproof case. Both need to be investigated. A short discussion could bring out both points and provide a focus for the work to avoid this being a construction project.

As a simple solution, a plastic bag might be tried. But is the seal at the top waterproof? Does it stay waterproof for very long? Does it remain sealed in use? Here are several opportunities to test the waterproofing in use.

The waterproof case must not affect the picture taken, so the amount of distortion that the plastic bag introduces needs to be determined in a qualitative manner. Pupils will need a simple one lens model of a camera to test, with the position of the lens, eyepiece and shutter clearly noted. A gauze in front of a light source can provide a suitable object.

MATERIALS, SAFETY, TIME

- Plastic bags, sticky tape, bacon ties, string.
- Large beakers.
- Cobalt chloride paper.
- Polystyrene.
- Other transparent materials that pupils may choose.
- 10-20cm converging lens, metal gauze and lamp, small screen.

Timing: 1 - 2 hours

NATIONAL CURRICULUM ASSESSMENT OPPORTUNITIES

AT6	Level 4	SofA	b
AT15	Level 6	SofA	a
	Level 7	SofA	c

EXPLORATION: What nutrients does a plant need?

WAYS FORWARD

Some discussion of fertilisers would be advantageous, as part of the introduction to this exploration.

Pupils may need to be given help on the necessity of setting up a control. It should also be explained that the solutions they use should not be too concentrated. Optimum values can be obtained from the packets of commercially-available plant foods.

It is a good idea to look at the effect of *not* having one of the nutrients on the plant, ie using the complete culture minus one of the nutrients. This can be repeated for all of the nutrients.

Relate the appearance of the plants to the solution that they have been grown in - which nutrients were present and which were lacking. For example, nitrates are necessary for green and healthy growth. Pupils will need some help with the presentation of their results.

MATERIALS, SAFETY, TIME

- Sugar, salt, nitrate eg $NaNO_3(s)$, phosphate $NaPO_4(s)$, sulphate $Na_2SO_4(s)$.
- Compound fertiliser eg NPK.
- Test tubes.
- Seedlings, eg grass.
- Spatulas.

Timing: 1 hour to set up and 1 week to leave.

NATIONAL CURRICULUM ASSESSMENT OPPORTUNITIES

AT3   Level 7   SofA   a

EXPLORING SCIENCE

PLANTS AND TREES

EXPLORATION: Describe to others how plants spread.

WAYS FORWARD

Start with some class discussion on what dispersal is and why it is necessary.

The pupils should be allowed to examine seed types and to simulate wind (using hair dryers) or insects (using a paintbrush) to see which is the most likely method of dispersal.

Some groups may be encouraged to come up with ideas about small animals (squirrels or birds) and how they may aid dispersal.

Wind-dispersed seeds can be examined for shape and how the particular shape affects its movement through the air. A poster is a good method of presentation of pupils' findings. A class video could also be considered.

MATERIALS, SAFETY, TIME

- Different plants, flowers.
- Magazines or gardening books.
- Magnifying glasses (hand lenses).
- Hair dryers (if possible).
- Grass seeds and trees are excellent specimens.

Timing: 1 hour.

NATIONAL CURRICULUM ASSESSMENT OPPORTUNITIES

AT3   Level 4   SofA   d

EXPLORATION: Show that plants need carbon dioxide.

WAYS FORWARD

This could be carried out after the exploration on testing a leaf for starch, starch being a product of photosynthesis.

Most pupils will want to see what happens to a leaf if carbon dioxide is not present. There is no observable difference in the leaf over the short term. Pupils may need to be encouraged to carry out the starch test.

Encourage pupils to set up a control leaf, eg one with KOH pellets (KOH absorbs the carbon dioxide) or possibly one where the plant gets enriched carbon dioxide from $NaHCO_3$

They will not be able to measure the amount of CO_2 in the air!

MATERIALS, SAFETY, TIME

- Geranium plants (one plant is not required).
- Potassuim hydroxide pellets.
- Clear plastic bags.
- Lime water.

Safety: KOH is caustic.

Timing: 1/2 hour to set up, 3 days to leave.

NATIONAL CURRICULUM ASSESSMENT OPPORTUNITIES

AT3   Level 6   SofA   b

PLANTS AND TREES

EXPLORATION: Design a test to show that leaves contain starch.

WAYS FORWARD

Pupils will firstly need to find a test for pure starch. They will probably do this by adding different chemicals to starch to see if there is any change.

They may then carry out the same test on a leaf.

Pupils should be encouraged to find a way of removing the waxy layer and the green colour. Do not allow direct heating of ethanol with a naked flame.

As an extension, pupils could carry out the test on variegated leaves.

MATERIALS, SAFETY, TIME

- Iodine solution, droppers.
- White tile.
- Ethanol.
- Boiling tubes, glass beaker, tripods, gauges.
- Bunsen burners.
- Starch solution or powder.
- Spotting tiles.

Safety: Ethanol is flammable.

Timing: 1 1/2 hours.

NATIONAL CURRICULUM ASSESSMENT OPPORTUNITIES

AT3   Level 6   SofA   b

PLANTS AND TREES

EXPLORATION: 'Most flowers are blue'. Show that this isn't true.

WAYS FORWARD

There are two approaches which can be taken to this exploration:
- An examination of flowers in their natural habitat. This could include quadrating to work out the *proportion* of flowers that are blue. The colours in question should all be those which occur naturally.
- Using books on flowers, gardening magazines, etc. (Naturally occuring and cultivated flowers.)

Pupils could be reminded that rare flowers should not be cut or picked.

If the answer to the exploration is 'no' then a question which could be asked is, "What are the most common colours?" ·

Small group discussions should follow concerning the colour of the flower in relation to the mode of pollination, ie blue, white and yellow flowers attract insects.

As an extension, investigate the shapes of flowers in relation to the ability of the flower to be insect pollinated.

MATERIALS, SAFETY, TIME

- Books, magazines, etc on flowers and plants.
- Available flower specimens.
- Meter rules.

Timing: 1 hour.

NATIONAL CURRICULUM ASSESSMENT OPPORTUNITIES

AT3   Level 4   SofA   d

PLANTS AND TREES

EXPLORATION: How would you arrange the plants?

WAYS FORWARD

Before starting this exploration, it may be necessary to name the different parts of a plant. Keys could then be used to identify the plants shown in the pupil's book. This will require pupils to use observable features of the plants.

Pupils could discuss in small groups the ways in which the plants could possibly be classified, eg:
- colour
- climbers
- conifers
- leaf shapes/colours,etc
- shapes of flowers.

Smaller detail of the plants can be investigated using a hand lens.

As an extension, pupils could do labelled diagrams of plants and/or dissect flowers and name all the parts.

MATERIALS, SAFETY, TIME

- Various plants or pictures of plants from magazines.
- Hand lenses.
- Keys for naming the plants.

Timing: 1 hour.

NATIONAL CURRICULUM ASSESSMENT OPPORTUNITIES

AT2   Level 3   SofA   a,b
        Level 5   SofA   b

EXPLORATION: How much air can a balloon hold?

WAYS FORWARD

Start with small group discussions on:
- What is volume?
- How can you measure volume?
- How can you measure the size and thickness of the balloon?

Make sure that pupils fully understand the concepts of volume, thickness and shape. A discussion about air being a mixture of gases may be useful at this stage.

Most pupils will try to measure the size of the balloon by using a tape measure, or a piece of tape and a ruler. They may need guidance to realise that the displacement of water is a valid way of finding the volume of air in the balloon.

Conclude by discussing which factors are dependent variables (ie size, thickness of rubber, temperature, shape) and which are independent variables (ie colour).

As an extension, pupils could try estimating the number of balloons from an assorted pack which could be filled from one 8000L cylinder. Or, using secondary sources, they could study atmospheric pressure and the work of Pascal.

MATERIALS, SAFETY, TIME

- Balloons of different shapes, sizes and colours, with thick and thin rubber.
- Tanks, bowls or sinks for water.
- Measuring cylinders (large ones!).
- Tape measures or rulers.
- Straws or tubing.

Timing: 1 hour.

NATIONAL CURRICULUM ASSESSMENT OPPORTUNITIES

AT1	Level 4	SofA	e
	Level 5	SofA	b
AT6	Level 6	SofA	e
AT17	Level 6	SofA	b

AT THE SEASIDE

EXPLORATION: How can you best grow plants in sand?

WAYS FORWARD

Pupils should start by comparing the growth rate of seeds in sand and in other types of soil (ie sand + ?). Pelargonium seeds would be suitable to use.

They will need to investigate the properties of sand, in particular its ability to retain water. They may need help in devising a scheme which will allow water to drip into sand and into other types of soil (sand + ?) at the same rates.

Microscopes can be used to examine soil and sand particles.

As an extension, using secondary sources, pupils could investigate how sand and soil are formed. A discussion on humus and drainage may prove valuable.

MATERIALS, SAFETY, TIME

- Pelargonium or other appropriate seeds (Mustard and cress seeds are not appropriate as they will grow in almost anything as long as there is water.)
- Test tubes or Petri dishes (or plant pots or yoghurt pots).
- Clear tubing.
- Compost, soil, straw, strips of paper.
- Stop clocks.
- Microscopes.

Timing: 1 week approximately.

NATIONAL CURRICULUM ASSESSMENT OPPORTUNITIES

AT3   Level 6   SofA   b
AT9   Level 3   SofA   d

EXPLORATION: What is the best size and shape for a sunshade?

WAYS FORWARD

Pupils should be encouraged to draw around the shadows that are made by the sunshade and to relate the size of the shadows to the distance or height that the sunshade is from the ground.

The experimental work should show:
- The effect of the surface area of the sunshade and height from the ground on the size of the shadow.
- How the light travels from the light source, bearing in mind the types of shadows it casts if a sunshade is obstructing it.

Discuss with pupils the positioning of the sun shade as the sun moves. Use the lamp as a model for the sun. This can be related to the daily movement of the sun.

The selection of the most suitable sunshade is largely governed by shape but other factors such as materials, cost and ease of carrying may also be important factors.

MATERIALS, SAFETY, TIME

- Lamps.
- Card, paper.
- Plasticine to hold up the sunshades.
- Matchsticks.
- Thin kitchen cloths, or any other material which could be used for making sunshades.

Timing: 1 hour.

NATIONAL CURRICULUM ASSESSMENT OPPORTUNITIES

AT15 Level 4   SofA   b

AT THE SEASIDE

EXPLORATION: Which goes bad quicker - sea water or tap water?

WAYS FORWARD

Discuss the following points with the pupils;
• How will we know if the water has gone off? (smell, slime)
• What could cause the water to go off?
• Is it something already in the water or something in the air?
• How can we find out?

Help may need to be given if pupils are to realise that salt is not the only difference between sea water and tap water. The tap water has been treated. How?

A fair test could be set up using:
• Tap water.
• Tap water + salt.
• Sea water (rain water + salt will do).

This exploration could lead on to looking at why water is impure, how water is treated, what the health risks are, etc.

As an extension, some pupils may be allowed to investigate the effects of adding bleach or disinfectants to the water.

MATERIALS, SAFETY, TIME

• Tap water.
• Salt water (note that the salt water should not be made of salt + tap water. Rain water is better).
• Petri dishes.
• Sodium hypochlorite solution (bleach).

Safety: Care must be taken if bleach is used.

Timing: 1/2 hour for setting up. 1-2 weeks for observations.

NATIONAL CURRICULUM ASSESSMENT OPPORTUNITIES

| AT5 | Level 5 | SofA | a |
| | Level 6 | SofA | a |

EXPLORATION: How big is a grain of sand?

WAYS FORWARD

Initiate small group discussion on:
- What is meant by 'big'?
- What measurements could be made?
- What would be the 'best' way to measure?
- The relative merits of length, mass and volume as measurements.

When measuring length, most pupils will attempt to measure the size of a grain by placing it alongside a ruler, but they may need guidance to take the next step, ie to see how many grains fit in 1mm. This procedure could be carried out using a microscope.

An alternative strategy may be to find the grain size by sieving the sand and finding the size of particles that do not pass through the mesh.

Difficulty may occur when it proves impossible to measure the mass of one grain of sand. Pupils may need help to proceed further and find how many grains of sand are in the smallest measurable unit on the balance. This problem may also occur when volume is measured.

Extension activities could lead into properties of sand and sugar, eg solubility. Pupils may wish to compare the appearance, ie colour and crystalline nature, as well as their size and mass. Extension work could also lead into ideas of estimating and distribution of grain size.

MATERIALS, SAFETY, TIME

- Builders' sharp sand - large particle size.
- Ruler.
- Top-pan balance or other accurate balance.
- Hand lenses/magnifying glasses/microscopes.
- Sieves with fine mesh.
- Sugar.
- Small volume measuring cylinders.

Timing: 1 hour.

NATIONAL CURRICULUM ASSESSMENT OPPORTUNITIES

AT6   Level 4   SofA   a

AT THE SEASIDE

EXPLORATION: What is the best shape for a wind break?

WAYS FORWARD

Start with small group discussion of what a good wind break does.

Pupils should then be encouraged to experiment with different types of materials to build the wind break. The shape of the wind break, its portability, cost, strength, ability to stand up, should all be examined.

Is there a wind speed after which the wind break is no good? Does the direction of the wind break have an effect?

Sand trays can be used to simulate the beach. Make sure the sand is wet so that pupils do not end up with sand in their eyes. Hair dryers can be used to simulate wind. Hair dryers with different speeds are ideal.

As an extension, the particulate model of air could be investigated. Investigate - wind is air in motion.

MATERIALS, SAFETY, TIME

- Hair dryers.
- Sand trays.
- Matchsticks/lollipop sticks/splints.
- Different types of materials, eg: paper, polythene, material of different weaves, metal sheets, etc.

Timing: 1-2 hours.

NATIONAL CURRIICULUM ASSESSMENT OPPORTUNITIES

AT9   Level 4   SofA   a
AT10 Level 7   SofA   b

THE SCRAPYARD

EXPLORATION: Make the best electromagnet for a crane.

WAYS FORWARD

Pupils need to know that an electromagnet is constructed from a coil and operates when electricity flows in the coil. Using paper clips or plotting compasses, the strength of the electromagnet can be quantified. Changes to the current, number and arrangement of coils, and the introduction of a core, can be compared with the original set up.

Current measurement may not be relevant at this time for some pupils. They can use the potential difference setting as a measure of the flow of electricity.

Many pupils will question the use of a core. Opportunity must be provided to investigate the effects of different cores. Toilet roll centres are useful to provide an air core. The addition of iron inside this will increase the strength of the electromagnet. This should be contrasted with non-ferromagnetic materials such as wood.

Pupils should be dissuaded from trying to build a complete crane, as the construction of the frame is not important in this exploration. A simple model can be made with a retort stand.

In fact, commercial crane magnets are made with permanent magnets and the electromagnet is used to allow the material picked up to be dropped, by opposing the polarity of the permanent magnet. This is for safety reasons in case of current failure while lifting.

MATERIALS, SAFETY, TIME

- Wire.
- Variable voltage dc power supply.
- Crocodile clips.
- Cardboard tubes.
- Iron rods, other metal and wooden rods.
- Paper clips.
- Magnets.
- Plotting compasses.

Safety: Large currents are needed to make strong electromagnets. These will heat up wires and will probably trigger the fuse in the power supply if left on for any time.

Timing: 2 hours.

NATIONAL CURRICULUM ASSESSMENT OPPORTUNITIES

AT11	Level 4	SofA	a
	Level 5	SofA	a,b
	Level 6	SofA	c
	Level 7	SofA	a

THE SCRAPYARD

EXPLORATION: How strong are the things we use?

WAYS FORWARD

Get pupils to bring in items that have been broken because their structure is damaged. These can then be considered, to discover where they broke and whether there is any discernible pattern in where objects break. Look particularly at the joints.

Pupils then need to test some objects. Plastic cutlery is reasonably cheap and can provide suitable objects to test.

Pupils should discuss in small groups how the object is usually used, to decide on a testing method that mirrors this use and allows a quantitative exploration.

Things to consider are:
- the size and point of application of the loads likely to be involved.
- the manner of loading.
- the speed of application of such forces.

The broken ends can be inspected, perhaps magnified, to determine the type of break. Is it repairable? Do the broken parts fit back together?

Transparent plastic models placed in polarised light and stressed, show brightly coloured patterns which can be used to determine where large stresses are.

MATERIALS, SAFETY, TIME

- Plastic cutlery.
- Other cheap items such as paper and card.
- Examples of broken artifacts.
- Weights.
- Newton meters.
- String, glue.
- Blocks of wood.
- Clamps.
- Safety glasses.

Safety: Sharp edges often result and pupils must be aware of this.

Timing: 1 hour.

NATIONAL CURRICULUM ASSESSMENT OPPORTUNITIES

AT10	Level 5	SofA	b,c
	Level 6	SofA	c

THE SCRAPYARD

EXPLORATION: How clean can an oily rag be made?

WAYS FORWARD

Start with small group discussion on:
- What is meant by clean?
- How might one measure how clean a rag is? Perhaps the question "How clean does it need to be?" would be a better one to ask.

What types of cleaner might be used? This could lead to a discussion about the environmental effects of cleaning materials. It should be a matter which is indicated as a possible problem at some time during the exploration.

The cost of cleaning against replacing the rag also matters. If the cost per cm^3 was on the container of cleaner, then pupils could estimate the costs for each type of cleaner.

Pupils might try to decide on a comparison with a clean rag, to decide how well the oil has been removed. Others might opt for a reflection of light method, if a suitable light sensitive cell were offered. Examination under magnification would also prove valuable. Essentially the process is one of judgement. A letter to a washing powder manufacturer would be useful to establish their methods of testing the cleaning ability of a washing powder.

Pupils might like to see who can clean a rag for the least cost. This would encourage a frugal use of the materials.

Portions of rag need to have the same degree of staining. Other variables which can be controlled are: the time the rag is cleaned for; the amount of cleaning agent used; the temperature and volume of water, if used.

MATERIALS, SAFETY, TIME

- Oily rags.
- Variety of cleaning agents.
- Hot and cold water, thermometer, timing clocks.
- Buckets, bowls, measuring cylinders, beakers.
- Hand lenses, microscopes.
- ORP 12 light dependent resistor in series circuit with 1.5 V cell and microammeter.

Safety: Disposable plastic gloves can be used to eliminate the possibility of some cleaning materials reacting adversely with some pupils' skin.

Timing: 1 hour.

NATIONAL CURRICULUM ASSESSMENT OPPORTUNITIES

AT1	Level 4	SofA	e
AT6	Level 9	SofA	b
AT8	Level 4	SofA	a

THE SCRAPYARD

EXPLORATION: Design a can crusher.

WAYS FORWARD

It would be tempting to crush cans by hand or foot. Pupils will need to be reminded that the scrapyard will have to deal with a large number of cans and will need some sort of crusher. Also, it can be pointed out that crushed cans could have very sharp edges and these could be dangerous if hand crushing were used.

The can crusher should make a significant reduction in the volume occupied by the cans. Pupils could choose to measure the volume of one can, and many will measure the volume a can contains, but it would be more sensible to measure the volume of a pile of cans, perhaps 10 in a plastic sack.

The can crusher could simply be a pair of jaws made from wood. It is important to emphasise that the crushed volume needs to be compared with the uncrushed volume.

The force needed to crush a can has to be measured to compare different cans and different methods of crushing. The results could be recorded in a table or bar chart.

MATERIALS, SAFETY, TIME

- Cans (useful to clear up the school grounds!).
- Wood, screws, hinges, string, nails.
- Weights, newton metres, rulers.
- Plastic bags.
- Cans for displacement method of volume measurement.
- Sticky tape, scissors.

Safety: Clearly there are possible dangers with sharp and rusty can and pupils will need to be aware of the need to take care. Cloths could be used to handle the cans if this was thought to be a difficulty.

Timing: 1 hour upwards.

NATIONAL CURRICULUM ASSESSMENT OPPORTUNITIES

AT1	Level 3	SofA	f
AT6	Level 4	SofA	a,b
AT10	Level 3	SofA	a
	Level 4	SofA	d

THE SCRAPYARD

EXPLORATION: Are some ways of making a fence better than others?

WAYS FORWARD

This is clearly a very open-ended piece of work. Pupils might first decide what tasks a fence has to perform. Some reasons for a fence that might emerge are:

- To keep something out.
- To keep something in.
- To hide an area from view.
- To shield from the wind.
- To mark a boundary.
- To look attractive.
- For security against intruders.

The reason for the fence needs to be made explicit by the fence builder, so that the fence can be tested to see if it performs its function well.

The testing of the fence needs to be arranged. This could involve the method of fixing the fence to the ground, although this might not be considered as a good test. If pupils had to span a fixed gap, say 10cm, then the ends of the fence section could be fixed and the test applied. Pupils might pull the fence with weights over a pulley or use a newton meter to pull the fence.

A record of the work could be a set of instructions to allow future fence structures to be tested in the same manner.

For a long-term view of the need for a good fence, pupils might gauge the effects of weathering on different structures. The variety of weather patterns would need to be known. Extreme storm conditions would be interesting to test, though difficult to arrange!

MATERIALS, SAFETY, TIME

- Wooden slats, wooden splints, twigs.
- Small stones.
- Copper wire.
- Glue, card, string.

Timing: 2 hours to allow time for building and testing.

NATIONAL CURRICULUM ASSESSMENT OPPORTUNITIES

AT1	Level 3	SofA	i
AT9	Level 4	SofA	b
AT10	Level 6	SofA	c
	Level 7	SofA	b

THE SCRAPYARD

EXPLORATION: How does a speaker make sound?

WAYS FORWARD

This exploration can be treated as a circus to allow all pupils to have access to limited apparatus as described below. Unfortunately, speakers do not produce good sounds at 50Hz, which is easily available from power supplies in Labs. This can form one station in the circus, and can be compared to the sounds produced by touching and removing a dc supply, no more than 3V.

The next station can use a signal generator to produce sounds from a speaker. The effect of varying the frequency can be investigated.

The magnetic field around the speaker can be investigated with a plotting compass. This would be carried out without a need to create sound.

The effect/need for the paper cone can be investigated by either cutting or, less destructively, by attaching pieces of plasticine to the cone. The cone is needed to allow a large volume of air to be moved by the speaker.

A useful partial replacement for a signal generator is a pre-prepared tape and a tape recorder. This can be used to investigate the sound at various angles from the speaker in the tape recorder. A microphone and an oscilloscope can be used to display the amplitude. Keep the volume low to keep interference with other groups to a minimum and to reduce the effects of reflection. Able candidates will realise that the distance from speaker to microphone needs to be kept constant and that arcs of sound are to be investigated.

Pupils should be encouraged to discuss their findings with the rest of the class. Perhaps a poster on *The Loudspeaker* could be developed to summarise the results of each group.

MATERIALS, SAFETY, TIME

- Several loudspeakers (these can be obtained from unwanted radios or stereo equipment).
- Two signals generators.
- Plotting compass.
- Iron filings.
- Plasticine.
- Scissors.
- Power supplies and leads.
- Crocodile clips.
- Tape recorder with 100Hz sound for about 2 minutes.
- Microphone.
- Oscilloscope.

Timing: 15 minutes in total for each part, 1 hour in total.

NATIONAL CURRICULUM ASSESSMENT OPPORTUNITIES

AT12	Level 3	SofA	a
AT14	Level 5	SofA	a,b
	Level 6	SofA	c

MATERIALS BOOK 1

SORTING THINGS OUT

SUMMARY

The book starts with an attempt to provoke discussion about the real characteristics of metals, in order to sharpen pupils' thinking. The topic goes on to examine non-metals as well, examining characteristic properties by the use of data tables and much experimental work. An Alien is used as interlocutor, to encourage pupils to be precise in their descriptions of properties and to recognise absurdities. The content is closely based on the National Curriculum. The three Materials are intended to subsume the entire National Curriculum requirements. The content of Book 3 overlaps into Key Stage 4 and will be appropriate for the more able student.

Sorting things out (page 1)

A deliberately provocative beginning, so that pupils realise that metals are recognised by a combination of properties. They may also come to see that the distinction between metallic and non-metallic behaviour represents a continuum, not an obvious sharp division.

Floating and sinking (page 2)

The purpose of the floating experiment is to link with the previous reference to the Titanic, ie that shape is crucial, not just relative density. The second experiment needs empty film cassette boxes weighted with sand or plasticine to achieve the effect illustrated.

Volume, mass and density (pages 2-3)

This is a very difficult area for many students and it is approached using thought experiments, a data table and class experiments. The scientific unit cm^3 is used in preference to the commercial ml.

Pupils will need advice as to the required degree of accuracy for the experiment at the top of page 3, eg to the nearest g or 0.1g for mass. The idea of experimental error, or *acceptable* range of divergence in results, could be discussed here.

The purpose of the data table is to provide unambiguous data to show which materials have densities greater than water (greater than $1g/cm^3$. The range of materials could be usefully extended following suggestions made by the pupils. The variability of the density of water with temperature has been ignored.

A proper shiner? (page 4)

Appropriate samples to use might include: aluminium cooking foil; cutlery; coins (new and old); wood (teak and varnished or painted); glass; plastics and a selection of fabrics. The concept of lustre is widely used in geology to differentiate minerals and rocks.

Bending and shaping (page 4)

Safety:

Warn about care with hot glass, both in terms of touching and the necessity to place hot glass on a heat-resisting mat. Safety glasses are essential.

The glass, being a sodium compound (soda glass) gives a yellow/orange sodium flame colour. The glass softens and bends under its own weight. If scrap material is available, try heating in the centre of the rod and pulling to give a glass fibre or joining pieces together. Further extensions could include discussion of: glass animals; blowing glass bottles; float-glass for windows; double glazing; Roman glass; natural glass obsidian — all as library-based projects.

Glass breaks with a conchoidal (shell-like) fracture with curved, sharp edges. It is particularly obvious with thick sheets. The idea of brittle behaviour and reversibility of bending (eraser, metals) can be discussed here.

Wires, fabrics and fibres (pages 5-6)

Test 5A

Weak fibres or a very strong balance are needed to give a range of results, or all fibres will produce the maximum scale reading.

Test 5B

Add masses and note the extension, perhaps until breaking point. Display results as a graph. Try removing masses one at a time to test reversibility. Compare rubber band, thin copper wire, nylon thread.

Safety:

Care should be taken when the breaking point is reached.

Extend this topic to discuss the uses of reversible elasticity, in clothes, 'octopus' holders for roof racks, and spiders' webs.

Test 5C

Try sharp and blunt-ended nails, and different heights. Look for the first evidence that the fabric has been pierced. Results can be displayed as a histogram, summarising different groups' findings. Try various papers, rubber balloon, plastic bag, clingfilm, aluminium cooking foil.

Test 5D

Use large samples of fabric or small samples with a solid surround, to avoid the air stream leaking around the edges.

Test 5E

Try both natural dyes (beetroot, litmus) and commercial dyes, with and without the mordant (for example, from alum and lime water). Test for colour fastness by washing or placing in sunlight (several weeks). Extend by considering fabric labels on clothes, dark colours, denim and bleached denim.

Safety:

Use safety glasses when heating and using mordant. Avoid skin contact by using tongs/ gloves.

Sheets and foils (pages 6-8)

A hand lens, stamp lens, or low power microscope are all suitable. Compare different types of paper, including filled paper from glossy magazines where the interstices contain china clay. Discuss the likely outcome of attempting to form sheets from the collage materials. Try also alternative strategies such as gelatine poured into a flat shallow dish instead of a jelly mould; practical work on plasticine, pastry, papier mache to produce the thinnest coherent sheet.

When testing the strength of materials, emphasise the importance of fair testing and ensuring that certain variables are kept constant.

Test 7A
The Bridge Test. Make predictions about maximum mass before the experiment.

Test 7B
The Breaking Test. Try newspaper, tissue, file paper and tracing paper. Display results on a histogram.

Test 7C
The Denting Test. Use large ball bearings or marbles and look for the first permanent dent.

Test 7D
The Twist Test. Use a G-clamp to fix one end and count the maximum number of twists.

The section at the top of page 8 presents opportunities for open-ended work on the strengths of structures such as bridges or towers.
Safety:
Warn about the danger of collapse when testing with house bricks.

Hard facts (pages 8-9)

Natural minerals can be tested for relative hardness using Mohs' scale. It is a non-linear scale, the difference in hardness between 1 and 2 differing from that between 2 and 3, and so on. For example, the difference between corundum (9) and diamond (10) is three times greater than the difference between talc (1) and corundum (9). It is a useful rule of thumb, but does not give absolute hardness values. Crystals often have different hardness values on different crystal faces. Gypsum is the crystalline version of plaster and Calcite that of chalk/limestone. Sand is composed of quartz. Granite often has crystals of quartz (glassy) and Feldspar (eg orthoclase) large enough to test for hardness. Many kerbstones are made of granite. The unglazed back of ceramic tiles provides a useful test plate; anything softer, like a graphite pencil "lead", leaves a mark on the tile.

Does hardness ever change? (pages 9-10)

Relate the nail experiment to the tempering of steel, and blacksmiths. Test also by clamping one end and trying to bend the nail using pliers. Look for surface colour changes.
Safety:
Warn about the danger of burns.

The Plaster of Paris can be carried out by comparing the difficulty of stirring or removing a plastic spoon, or try inverting the container. Comment on the heat given out on setting, which is evidence of a chemical reaction.

Conduction of heat (page 10)

With the copper strip, the wax melts very rapidly indeed. Warn pupils to watch closely. For iron use a file, and for clay, a strip from a ceramic tile. Compare the thickness of the materials in the context of a fair test. Both tile and glass could be held, but the metals need tongs.

Safety:
Burns warning. Wear safety glasses in case a strip shatters on heating.

Expansion (page 11)

For the pointer experiment, use a large diameter copper rod for the best effect, clamping the other end very securely. The pointer and roller could be made using balsa wood or a straw, placing a card scale behind it.

Safety:
Warn against placing a plastic-covered freezer pack on to a very hot copper rod.

Pendulum experiment: Try preliminary experiments with one pendulum length, such as varying the amount that it is pulled to one side before release. Also, show that the mass of the bob has no effect. Agree exactly what counts as one complete pendulum swing before accurate timing. The alloy invar does not expand significantly at ambient temperatures, hence its value in clock making.

The heat goes on (page 12)

Cooling experiment: This offers an opportunity for open-ended experiments on different insulators. Extend by discussions of everyday examples: cavity wall, loft, fur, duvet, clothing, sleeping bag.

Flame experiment: Cooling the gauze in a freezer immediately before use helps this experiment . Light gas *above* the gauze. Once the gauze warms up, the flame 'jumps' through to give a continuous flame. The use of gauzes was the basis of the Davy safety lamp for miners. For the candle experiment, the best results are obtained by using a candle stub (3-5cm) and thick wire. As the heat is conducted away, the flame is extinguished.

Electrical conductivity (page 13)

Test rig: Advise pupils to test the bell/buzzer/light before each new material. Extend by introducing the idea of circuit diagrams and shorthand symbols.

Safety:
Warn pupils not to try this at home using mains supply.

The trouble with water (pages 13-15)

Rusting experiment 14A: Most children seem to expect the mass to decrease during the week. The reverse comes as a surprise. The picture equation is sufficient for many to realise why this happens. Extend by consideration of size changes such as rusting reinforcement bars splitting concrete or stone. Emphasise the point that rust flakes away from solid iron to release a fresh surface for corrosion to continue.

Rusting experiment 14C: The water level should rise by 1/5, leaving nitrogen gas behind. The rise is rarely exact, but the remaining gas can be shown to be depleted in oxygen since a burning splint is rapidly extinguished.

When a glass of cold water is left overnight, bubbles of previously dissolved air appear as the cold water in the glass warms up to ambient temperature.   Extend by discussion of the connection between solubility and temperature, ie that solids become more soluble as the temperature rises (but not salt), whereas gases become less soluble. A consideration of the sounds made by the water in an electric kettle long before it boils should get pupils to suggest that dissolved air is being expelled as the temperature rises.

The Rust Olympics (pages 15-16)

Since both air and water are required, and rusting is accelerated by electrolytes such as salt, the result should be clear. Use calcium chloride as a drying agent. A transparent plastic tray or one sealed with clingfilm is best for the comparative experiment using other metals. Extend by a discussion of exactly what metal is involved since, for example, most paper clips and drawing pins are plated steel (iron).

Page 16: Everyday examples of surface corrosion will be familiar to most pupils. Silver tarnishes by reaction with hydrogen sulphide, as does copper, in addition to reaction with air and water. Bad eggs release the gas hydrogen sulphide. Why is there no rust on the iron railings? The order of reactivity is; iron, copper, silver, gold.

Discuss ways of preventing corrosion, such as:
- exclude water (desert).
- coat the surface with another metal (tin or zinc).
- alloy with another metal (stainless steel = iron + nickel + chromium).
- paint.
- enamel.

Families of elements (pages 17-18)

The National Curriculum emphasises the importance of this topic and the opportunity is taken in Materials Book 1 to introduce a few chemical symbols whilst investigating the periodicity of some properties.

Alkali metal reactions: These demonstration reactions can be seen well using an OH Projector and covered Petri dishes. Pieces of metal about 3-4mm across are adequate. The addition of a few drops of phenolphthalein indicator produces purple trails behind the reacting metals. The reactivity sequence is clear, with lithium the least and potassium the most reactive. It is worth relating the name alkali metals to the production of alkalis such as sodium hydroxide in the Petri dishes, hence the purple colour. This point is brought out in the class experiment with indicators.

Safety;
Use small pieces of alkali metals, handle with tongs and wear safety glasses. Use safety screens.

It is not intended that the experiments on page 18 be demonstrated, as they are too dangerous in an open laboratory. Extend by discussion of the uses of inert gases, such as diving mixture (helium/oxygen), neon lights, argon in filament bulbs.

Oxides (page 18)

This is to emphasise the names of the compounds derived from oxygen. Although formulae are given, it is not possible to justify them at this stage.

Electrolysis (page 19)

Testing liquids: Use strong solutions, saturated or nearly so, for best results. The filter paper strip could be supported on a microscope slide with the electrodes/crocodile clips close together. Use 6-8 volts dc. Suitable liquids could include:
- potassium bromide (brown colour of bromide).
- potassium iodide (brown colour of iodine.
- potassium iodine/starch solution (blue colour).

Y-shaped paper experiment: Nothing happens whilst the paper remains dry. Mark + and - in pencil on the paper. Either wait until the liquid soaks up or dip the paper in the solution and then allow 6-8 volts to run. Copper sulphate gives a blue colour on the - side. Potassium chromate gives a yellow on the + side.

The advantage of using the OH Projector is that it becomes obvious that chemical changes occur only at the electrodes.

Distilled water   - no change since no charged ions are present.

Salt water   - bubbles of gas, chlorine on + side. Add some indicator for the chlorine to bleach.

Copper sulphate - brown copper on - side.

Sulphuric acid   - bubbles of gas, hydrogen on - and oxygen on + side.

Extend to non-aqueous liquids like alcohol or paraffin (no result) or to familiar materials like lemonade or soda water (gases produced).

Foreign coins are suggested to avoid a charge of defacing the coinage. Clean the coin with soapy water, distilled water, then alcohol and avoid touching the cleaned surface.

When did people first use metals? (page 20)

The historical order of use of materials for weapons and tools does not reflect their abundance in nature, but rather their ease of extraction. Aluminium is the commonest metal in the Earth's crust, but it requires large amounts of electricity and is therefore very much a 20th century metal. The other main point to emphasise is the occurrence of native metals, in a pure form, reflecting their lack of chemical reactivity. The commonest are gold, silver, copper and mercury. Ores (chemical compounds) of the latter three also occur naturally.

Extend by links with local museums and books dealing with the uses of gold and bronze, such as in ancient Egypt or Greece, together with modern uses in coins or microelectronics.

Ore minerals are extracted for their economic importance. The waste ones are gangue minerals. In the 19th century, uranium minerals were regarded as gangue minerals, but are now of value for nuclear power.

Alloy, Alloy! (pages 20-22)

Extend the information on alloys by a library search:
- What percentage of each metal is there in particular alloys?
- When was stainless steel discovered, and how?
- What metals are there in other alloys such as gun metal, bell metal, type metal, pewter?
- What is the difference between iron and steel?

Froth flotation is an efficient method of concentrating the metal content of low-grade ores. Use water with a little disinfectant added, finding best proportions by experiment. For a sample ore, mix sand (gangue mineral = waste) with some powdered metal compound such as iron sulphide, and use zinc sulphide to represent the valuable ore. Graphite powder (from pencil 'leads') could also be used. The ore minerals stick to the surfaces of the bubbles and rise to the top, leaving the waste behind. A mechanical sweeping arm then continuously removes the bubbles and attached ore particles for further treatment.

The flow diagram on page 22 is to emphasise the general pattern of iron extraction and its international nature as an industry.

Extend by comparing the small-scale inland iron works of the Industrial Revolution with the large, modern integrated industry located at or near a deep-water part. Slag is used for road base material and landfill, but much remains in unsightly slag-heaps. Discuss the related air and water pollution, together with the impact of limestone quarrying in areas of outstanding natural beauty such as Derbyshire.

Low grade ores (less than 1% metal) are increasingly being worked as better quality mineral deposits become exhausted. Discuss the implications:
- More expensive raw metals.
- Substitution, such as optical fibres for copper wires.
- Recycling, as with aluminium cans.

Non-metals (page 23)

Emphasise the dramatic change of properties caused by adopting a different crystal pattern. Diamonds can be made from graphite to produce industrial stones for drills and cutting tools. Gem quality stones are mined.

Extend by discussion of other uses:
- Carbon fibre in sports equipment.
- Carbon fibre in aeroengine blades.
- Diamonds in history, writing on glass.
- Graphite as a lubricant.

Carbon and silicon are both in Group 4 of the Periodic Table, but their oxides are very different. Carbon is unique. Extend to consider carbon in an organic context: the basis of life on Earth, petroleum and petrochemicals.

You can call me Al (page 24)

This considers aluminium extraction as a contrast to iron. Approximately 7% of the Earth's crust is aluminium, making it the commonest available metal in nature. Extend by a library search of the discovery and price of aluminium in the 19th century, comparable in value to gold.

Metal Mastermind (page 24)

Although other interpretations are possible, the assumptions made in preparing the table were:

A = an alkali metal such as lithium, sodium, potassium.
B = sulphur, a non-metal.
C = copper, hard by comparison with A.
D = graphite (carbon), the only non-metal to conduct electricity well.

Materials Book 1 offers the following National Curriculum Assessment Opportunities:

Attainment Target	Level	SofA	Pages
AT6	Level 3	a	20-22,24
		b	1-9,24
	Level 4	a	1,4-9
		b	4,6,8,11,21,23
		c	2,3
	Level 6	a	2-10,12,13,19,23
		c	18,23,24
		d	17,18
	Level 7	a	1,4-14
		b	6,11,16,20-22,24
		c	17,18
AT7	Level 4	a	13,15,18,19
		b	21,22,24
	Level 5	a	20-22
	Level 6	c	9,22

Attainment Target	Level	SofA	Pages
AT7	Level 7	b	18,22-24
		c	22,24
		d	15,16,21
AT8	Level 6	b	11
		c	18,23
	Level 7	c	23
AT10	Level 3	b	2
AT11	Level 7	b	19
AT13	Level 4	e	11
	Level 6	b	12

MATERIALS BOOK2

GASES

SUMMARY

This book follows on from the "Sorting things out" topic of Materials Book 1, to investigate the properties of gases. There is a concentration on an experimental approach, although the difficult topics of oxidation, combustion and respiration are included. The Alien interlocutor is used to show a little philosophical doubt and to push arguments to absurdities in order to encourage clear thinking by the pupils. Although some of the material will probably have been encountered at Key Stage 2, this book makes the transition to a truly scientific approach to investigations. Tests are established and applied and data is collected and displayed in a variety of ways to assist analysis.

Gases - are they really there at all? (pages 1-2)

Although the idea of 'pouring' gases from one container to another seems obvious, it is one that many pupils have not considered before. The experimental work should make it clear that words like 'empty' need to be qualified.

The seltzer experiment on page 2 is chosen to encourage close and accurate observation, making it clear that this is a skill central to science.

The experiments on moving gases, together with the illustrations, are to emphasise that pupils can call on their own experience to describe and account for scientific changes.
Safety:
Take care using a hair dryer near water.

The candle experiment dates back to the 17th century. As the oxygen content of the air is depleted, the water level inside rises. It is rare to get the 'right' answer of a 21% rise, corresponding to the oxygen content in air. An extension would be to consider why this is so: temperature changes; the solubility of the gases involved; experimental error, etc. Improvements could be tried: use a calibrated cover jar; take the average results of several experiments; try suspending the candle above the water level away from the carbon dioxide produced. The jar should contain nitrogen and carbon dioxide (and water vapour) at the end. Test with a burning splint to show that no oxygen remains. It will be extinguished.

As light as air? (pages 3-5)

For the gas preparation, use: carbon dioxide from marble chips and dilute hydrochloric acid; oxygen from 20volume hydrogen peroxide solution with a few mg of solid manganese IV oxide (manganese dioxide) added as a catalyst to speed up the reaction; hydrogen from dilute (2Molar) hydrochloric acid and a 2cm piece of magnesium ribbon.

All of these reactions are fast and the hydrogen production is accompanied by much heat as well.

The splint: continues at first in air; is extinguished in carbon dioxide; burns more brightly in pure oxygen; and 'pops' with a minor explosion with hydrogen.
Safety:
Safety glasses are essential.

The experiment with soap bubbles is fun if messy. The hydrogen bubble rises, the carbon dioxide sinks in air. Extend by modifying the bubbler (a clay-type pipe works well) to produce larger bubbles or by varying the detergent type or concentration.

The dense gas carbon dioxide can be poured over the enclosed candle to extinguish it. Extend by a consideration of commercial extinguishers and their applications.

Page 4: The balloon balance needs a pivot with low friction to be successful. Using a pin through a ruler may be better, although it needs to be drilled if it is to work well. Get the pupils to predict what will happen when gas escapes from one balloon. Try alternative, non-destructive, ways of releasing the gas, such as the small plastic taps used in filtering home-made wine. Natural gas is only slightly less dense than air, whilst carbon dioxide is much more dense. Extend by considering helium-filled balloons - the molecules are so small that they escape through the fabric even when perfectly sealed on filling.

Ask pupils to offer their own ideas of the composition of the air before moving on to the accepted values.

Testing the air (page 5)
The carbon dioxide test: The solution is calcium hydroxide, usually known as limewater (strong alkaline). It becomes cloudy in the presence of carbon dioxide gas. The cloudiness consists of solid particles of calcium carbonate, chemically the same as chalk or limestone. Eventually these particles redissolve if sufficient carbon dioxide is available, leaving a solution of calcium hydrogen carbonate, a hard water sample.

The water test: Cobalt chloride paper should be oven-dried before use. The word 'anhydrous' for copper sulphate has been replaced by dried, but either would be acceptable. This latter test is clearer, giving an unambiguous change from colourless to blue in the presence of water. Extend by testing other liquids for water content.

Shape and volume (page 6)
This starts with revision of the variability of shape of liquids which are moved to different containers. The important issue is to emphasise that gases spread to occupy the volume available to them, as is shown in the subsequent experiments.

Do gases behave like liquids? (pages 6-7)
The gas syringe needs a low-friction piston, glass ones work best. The decreasing volume of the fixed amount of gas as the added mass increases is clear. Before the temperature variation experiments, ask for predictions from the students. Use the analogy of a balloon placed in a freezer or on a radiator.

Since glass is a poor conductor, there is a delay before the piston moves on changing the temperature. To try the water-filled syringe experiment, use small plastic syringes for safety reasons.

Aerosol experiment: Make the point that the box also contains air and that the gas from the aerosol mixes with it. The evidence that gases spread (diffusion) to occupy the volume available, can be generalised from gases that you can smell (aerosol) to all gases.

The Great Gas Race (page 7)

This demonstration needs good ventilation. Results can take up to 20 minutes, depending on the length of the tube.

Use concentrated hydrochloric acid on one piece of cotton wool (tongs) and concentrated ammonia solution (0.88 ammonia) on the other. Pieces of universal indicator can be placed onto a length of copper wire. Show the pupils what happens when the opened bottles of the two reagents meet - white smoke forms. The ammonia is less dense and travels faster, so that the gases meet to give a smoke ring nearer to the hydrochloric acid end.

What are gases like? (page 8)

This simple model of the way that molecules behave, according to the kinetic theory, can be extended by considering everyday analogies such as snooker. The 'molecules' collide with each other and with the sides of the container. When different molecules are added, they diffuse into the existing gas and mix permanently. Petri dishes could be used for the containers.

The assembly of key words from those presented, serves to clarify the connection between motion of molecules and their energy.

Balloon experiments: The key idea is that the molecules colliding with the sides of the container produce the observed pressure of the gas, and hence the size of the balloon.

Cold breath (page 9)

Discuss this in terms of the exhaled molecules losing energy as they move to a colder environment outside the body.

Both the first example and the cold mirror surface represent the change of state of water molecules from vapour (invisible) to liquid as their energy falls. Emphasise that water vapour exists over a wide temperature range; relate it to evaporation from oceans and cloud formation.

What's the matter? (pages 10-12)

Thermometer experiment: Good results are only produced if stirring is continuous and the thermometer bulb is above the base of the beaker. Present the results as a graph or histogram, or draw on an OH Projector for discussion. Ask for predictions as to the likely result. Many will suggest a constant temperature rise. Ask for a description of what the pupils could see happening when the temperature was constant (during the change of state).

Extend the generalisation about temperature and changes of state by the subsequent experiments. The sample results are on page 11 to revise and clarify exactly how to recognise from a suitable graph that a change of state has occurred. Emphasise that the pupils are to look for a region where the temperature remains the same. Experiment A is the coffee.

Ring-pull can experiment: As the water freezes, the ice expands out of the hole. Prepare some cans before the lesson to save time, but regular pupil checks as freezing progresses are better. Extend by repetition at home with an estimate of the approximate volume change.

Polythene bag experiment: Use an electrical hotplate to avoid fire hazard. Extend by a consideration of steam engines, their history and applications. Experiments follow on page 13.

Sublimation experiment: Use dry tubes and hold them parallel to the bench so that the end becomes hot but the remainder of the glass stays cold. The ammonium chloride sublimes and crystals form on the cool glass.
Safety:
Safety glasses are essential.

Extend by asking how ammonium chloride could be separated from sand without using water, ie by sublimation.
Safety:
Beware of toxic fumes from the sublimation.

All steamed up (page 13)
Water can be soaked into glass wool at the closed end of the tube. Float the steamboat in a piece of domestic guttering or a large tray. For the turbine, try alternative blade designs and angles by cutting several turbines from foil dishes.
Safety:
Before trying the experiments, warn pupils about being burned by steam.

Gas power (page 14)
Book experiment: Introduce this by offering to blow over a pile of books and invite alternative strategies.

Catherine wheel: Locate the spindle through the wheel/dish into some plasticine on the base of a tray. Check for free movement before adding the seltzer tablet. Try different sizes and angles for the jet.

Syringe lift: Use this experiment to discuss the expansion of the gas in terms of energy gained by the molecules. Extend by considering the commercial applications of this technique. Are there any drawbacks?

Balloons: It will need several attempts to achieve the correct balance. Try releasing on a sloping smooth surface.

Plastic cup: The gas produced is carbon dioxide. Try alternative designs and power sources such as seltzer tablets.

Combustion (pages 15-17)
Close observation of the candle flame should produce a list - heat, light, water soot, change of state of the wax.

Candle investigation: At the start, there will be condensation on the cold glass funnel. The (anhydrous) copper sulphate turns blue eventually. It may need several uses of the syringe. The limewater goes cloudy with the carbon dioxide produced by combustion.

Word equation: Natural gas (methane) + air -> carbon dioxide + water vapour + soot (carbon) sometimes when combustion is incomplete.

Bunsen burner: Point out the similarity of the yellow candle flame to the yellow Bunsen flame, ie incomplete combustion gives luminous flames. The blowpipe changes the flame to blue as extra oxygen is added. A bicycle pump could be used instead of a blowpipe. Use this opportunity to discuss the composition of exhaled air, ie that it still contains oxygen.

Wires: The glowing nichrome wires show the hottest part of the flame to be above the central blue cone. Tapping into the blue cone shows it be to unburnt gas. The match remains cool in the gas stream and does not ignite.

Carbon monoxide: Emphasise that carbon monoxide contains less oxygen than carbon dioxide, as it is being formed in a restricted air supply. It is very poisonous.

The fire triangle (pages 17-18)
Ask for interpretations of fire-fighting techniques in terms of the triangle. Pupils should realise that water added to certain fires (fat or oil) exacerbates the situation, since the fuel floats and continues to burn.

Foam extinguishers contain bubbles of carbon dioxide which form a 'blanket' over the oil, preventing oxygen in the air from reaching the fire.

Model fire extinguisher: This experiment can be very messy but is worth the trouble. Use a solution of sodium carbonate or sodium hydrogen carbonate (bicarbonate), warmed slightly. Beware of using a narrow jet or the stopper will blow out. As an acid, ethanoic (acetic) is safest but a demonstration might use hydrochloric (with safety screens).
Safety:
Safety glasses are essential.

Combustion and respiration (pages 19-20)
Drawing the histogram emphasises the differences to the pupils.   At this stage, most will recognise the tests for gases:
Lime water - carbon dioxide.

Mirror - water vapour.
Bunsen - oxygen added from exhaled air.
Safety:
Take care with any pupil suffering from asthma or any similar condition.

Construct the word equation:
Fuel + oxygen -> water vapour + carbon dioxide + energy released.

Respiration: Respiration only occurs in living things. The temperatures involved in the two processes are very different.

Exhaled air and lung capacity: This is necessarily a rather crude measure of capacity. The jar needs to be large enough for the largest volunteer.

Does water contain air? (pages 20-21)
The apparatus must be completely filled with cold water. There should be no tubing projecting beneath the stopper or air bubbles will be trapped. Many pupils will suggest steam as the gas collecting but this provides an opportunity to discuss temperature effects. Measure the temperature of the collection tube. A burning splint continues to burn in the gas. It may be necessary to combine samples or repeat with a large-scale apparatus.

Make clear that the solubility of gases decreases as the temperature rises.

What *is* oxidation? (pages 21-23)
Oxide experiments: Iron filings produce sparks, very effective in a darkened room. Iron wool shows individual strands burning to leave solid iron oxide. Both magnesium and aluminium are potentially hazardous, owing to the brightness of the flames and the temperatures produced. Both oxides are white powders.
Safety:
Safety glasses are essential.
Pupils must realise that the oxide weighs more than the original metal.

Balance: The two problems are that insufficient air may enter to ensure complete combustion or that the fine oxide dust will escape before it can be weighed.

Candle burning: This can be a very fruitful source of ideas for discussion, since the mass decreases. Structured questioning will elicit the idea that the oxides formed escape, being gaseous, and could not be weighed easily.

Oxidation of food: Inert atmospheres (nitrogen or argon) or the absence of air (vacuum packing) stop oxidation.

Oxidation and colours: Present a selection of dyes and inks for comparison. Perhaps include newsprint (carbon), which is unaffected.
Safety:
Warn about the hazards of using bleach. Safety glasses are needed.

Reductions: Only bauxite and cassiterite are reductions. Emphasise that most commercially important metals are produced by the reduction of their oxides.

Fermentation - letting nature have a go (pages 23-24)

Temperature: Warm is best, since at high temperatures the yeast dies, whilst at low temperatures it become inactive. The fermentation can be slow to start, especially if granular yeast is used. Make up the yeast solution in advance. Extend by consideration of other uses of enzymes, as in biological washing powders.

Distillation: It is legal if on a small scale for scientific purposes. Better separation is achieved using a fractionating column attached to the distillation flask. Monitor the temperature and test the first few ml by igniting them in an evaporating basin to show that alcohol is present.

Alternatively, avoiding the use of ethanol, fractionate another liquid mixture to demonstrate the principle, say water and propanone (acetone - very flammable). Extend by consideration of alcohol fuels for the 21st century to replace oil-based fuels.

Consider the agricultural implications of alcohol production, that less land is available for food, etc.

Pollution: Discuss unburned fuel (hydrocarbons) and photochemical smog, smoke, lead in fuel, nitrogen oxides and the use of catalytic converters, electric cars and bicycles.

Extend to project work on fuel supplies and uses, together with alternative energy sources.

Materials Book 2 offers the following National Curriculum Assessment Opportunities:

Attainment Target	Level	SofA	Pages
AT3	Level 6	a	19,20
AT6	Level 4	a	20,21
		c	6
		d	9,10
		e	1,4,11,12
	Level 5	a	3,4
	Level 6	a	3,7,11,20
		e	6,8,12-14
AT7	Level 4	a	2,15-17,19-22
		b	3,23,24
	Level 5	a	23,24
		b	23,24
		c	15-17,19,20
	Level 6	c	15-17
	Level 7	a	23
		b	21,22
AT8	Level 4	a	8,10,11
	Level 5	a	8,9

Attainment Target	Level	SofA	Pages
AT8	Level 6	a	8,12
		b	6,8,11-14
		c	16,19,20,22
	Level 7	a	7,9,13
AT10	Level 3	a	14
	Level 4	a	14
AT13	Level 3	a	13
	Level 4	a	19,20
		b	18,24
		d	10,11,12
		e	10,11,12
	Level 5	a	24
		b	24
	Level 6	a	13

MATERIALS BOOK 3

ATOMS AND MOLECULES, SOLUTIONS AND IONS

SUMMARY

This third and final book dealing with the properties of materials, extends the treatment in a more abstract way. This will provide the theoretical groundwork required for Key Stage 4 and the GCSE courses in science. The book deals with the properties of atoms and molecules, together with the difficult topic of ions. As with Books 1 and 2, the emphasis is on experimental work with links, where appropriate, to the real world.

Model molecules (page 1)

Emphasise that the molecules or particles themselves remain unchanged even though there has been a change of state. In the model, the spheres need to be held in close contact so that there is no relative movement and they move as a single unit.

When the model is changed to be like water, the spheres are able to slide past one another. Try adding a few marked spheres and agitating the 'liquid' to show that molecules move about in liquids.

Molecules in motion (page 2)

Nail varnish remover: the liquid propanone (acetone) has a low boiling point and is very easily evaporated by the heat of the hand. Pupils should notice that the molecules disappear. A smell of the vapour can be detected, confirming that the molecules are in the gas phase, and the hand feels cold as the energy required is taken from it.

Hydrogen: Use granulated zinc and dilute 2M sulphuric acid. Reaction can be accelerated by adding a few drops of copper sulphate solution.
Safety:
Safety glasses are essential.
The hydrogen diffuses rapidly in all directions. All the tubes give a 'pop' test. Emphasise that molecules do not always follow the common sense rules. Here we have 'light' molecules moving downwards and vice versa. Diffusion means that all the various gas molecules, acting independently, spread out to occupy all the available volume.

Still water? (page 3)

At this early stage no attempt should be made to justify the atom ratio in formulae, whilst confidence is being built up in recognising the formulae. Extend by offering other formulae for analysis and using a quiz approach and flash cards.

Staying in shape (page 3)

The argument is now developed to show that molecules are not uniformly spherical but have a variety of shapes. This is only effective as practical work. Use drawings or plasticine or beads. It may be appropriate to introduce the appropriate prefix for some molecules such as tri- or tetra-. The illustrations show sulphur hexafluoride, hydrogen sulphide (bad egg gas) and the element sulphur with eight atoms in a ring-shaped molecule.

Let's stick together (pages 4-5)

Dust on water shows that surface tension (attraction between water molecules at the surface) is sufficient to prevent dust breaking through and sinking.

As the blotting paper becomes wet and sinks, the needle floats, Extend by considering pond skaters, Brownian motion, and trying other powders on water, such as sulphur powder.

Try adding a detergent dropwise to reduce the surface tension of the water. The needle sinks and the powders sink on stirring. Also, a water droplet on clean glass would begin to spread out.

Dropping funnel: This is a good demonstration experiment showing the equivalent of a dripping tap in slow motion. Any two immiscible liquids will work but salt water (dense) added to cooking oil works well. Adjust the tap to produce a very slow stream. Watch the formation of each drop, held in shape by surface tension, and the way it breaks away and coalesces at the base.

Capillary: There is an attraction between the glass surface and the molecules of the liquid. Extend by looking at polypropylene (polypropene) measuring cylinders where there is almost no interaction, glass cylinders where the edges go up (meniscus) and mercury in a sealed tube with an inverted meniscus.

Meths: Use a hot water bath and no naked flames nearby. The intermolecular attraction is less with molecules in meths (methanol), hence it boils at a lower temperature, about $65^{\circ}C$ for methanol and $78^{\circ}C$ for ethanol.

Molecules - what's the attraction? (page 5)

A very strong force meter is needed in the tensile strength experiment. For the twist test, either twist until it breaks or until no more turns are possible.

Plaster of Paris: Emphasise that heat energy is released, indicating the formation of links/ bonds between the particles as water is added. This topic is ideal for an extended investigation into modifying the properties of the basic material. Extend by considering the history of building materials, straw mixed with clay for bricks, the use of ovens for ceramics, etc.

Molecules all in a line (page 6)

Polymers: This must be a demonstration experiment and could be carried out under a glass container to minimise the escape of fumes. Make a saturated solution of urea (carbamide), pointing out the fall in temperature as it dissolves (an endothermic change). A total of 50ml will do. Add a solution of methanal (formaldehyde), 25m,l and stir. Add 1-2ml of concentrated sulphuric acid as a catalyst to accelerate the reaction and place a cover over the beaker. The urea-methanal plastic sets solid within 5 minutes.
Safety:
Take care with formaldehyde and fumes. Safety glasses are essential for the concentrated

sulphuric acid. Do *not* **use hydrochloric acid, as a carcinogen is formed.**

Human polymer: This is great fun if you dare to try it. For the crosslinking, get the pupils to join lines together.

Hot properties: Ask pupils to bring in old plastic containers and cut them up into pieces. Use very hot water and electrical heating to avoid fires. Emphasise that many plastics release toxic fumes on burning. For the oven, place objects on heat- resisting mats in the oven. Draw conclusions from the results, such as that the material for light fittings does not soften on heating.

More about polymers: This can be done as a 'circus' but pupils may already be familiar with some from Key Stage 2, for example floating/sinking.

When atoms and molecules meet (pages 7-8): The point to make is that when atoms and/or molecules combine together (chemical reaction), new materials with new properties are produced. Contrast this with the diffusion of gases where the molecules simply mix but do not react.

The sodium + chlorine experiment is too dangerous to try, but is worth discussing since two dangerous materials react to give salt.

Mistakes in formulae: Calcium chloride needs two chloride ions, aluminium needs three for electrical neutrality.

The ion snap game (page 9)
The ions have charges equal to their Group number (Groups 1 and 2) or (8 - their Group number) for Groups 6 and 7.   Obviously this is a very selective table and ignores exceptions.

The game is very effective in getting students to write and recognise correct ionic formulae but it can get very noisy. Four players are ideal.

The latest attractions (page 10)
Aluminium + iodine: Both powders should be finely ground, separately, and oven dried until needed. The addition of water catalyses the reaction to form aluminium iodide, releasing purple iodine vapour (toxic).
Safety:
Safety screen and glasses are essential, together with good ventilation.

Problems with solutions (page 10-11)
Revise the technical terms associated with solutions.

Fair test: Choose the soluble materials only and, using a fixed volume of water (10ml or 20ml), add weighted amounts and shake to dissolve, continuing until no more will dissolve (saturated solution). Check that the temperature remains constant; it may be necessary to warm or cool to ensure this.

Iodine: Avoid skin contact. This may be best as an assisted demonstration. It is soluble easily in nail polish remover (propanone/acetone).

Solubility experiment: Try 2, 4, 6, 8, 10, 12, 14 and 16 g of solid for different groups, using potassium nitrate. Warn pupils to avoid heating the water until it boils. The crystals reappear when the solution becomes saturated as the temperature falls. The graph shows that the solubility rises as the temperature rises. Remind pupils that this is the opposite way round to soluble gases like air in water.

Mixing solutions together (page 12)
This represents the process of double decomposition or ionic association, where the ions combine to give an insoluble product, leaving another new material in solution.

Experiment:
potassium chromate - yellow solution.
chalk - insoluble, leave to stand after stirring.
copper sulphate - blue solution.
benzoic acid - soluble only in hot water.
potassium manganate VII (permanganate) - purple solution. Extend by diluting until colour disappears; gives an indication of how many particles (ions in this case) were originally added.
sodium nitrate - colourless solution. Extend by vaporation to regain the solid iodine - (handle using tweezers for safety reasons), almost insoluble in water.
General note - use very small samples of solids in test tubes for best results.
The yellow solid is lead chromate, the solution contains potassium nitrate. Extend by filtration, washing and drying to give pure lead chromate (toxic) and evaporation to give crystals of potassium nitrate (colourless).

The convention is to write the name of the metal first when giving the name of the compound.

Are gases soluble in water? (page 13)
Unless they react with the water, most gases are not very soluble in water at normal pressures. Ammonia reacts and is therefore very soluble, carbon dioxide only slightly soluble. Build on the pupils' experience of fizzy drinks to emphasise the use of pressure to force gases into solution.

Experiment with solubility and temperature: A small amount of previously dissolved air collects.

Pure is sure (pages 13-16)
Useful points: Use single crystals in a dry capillary tube or melting point tube held against the thermometer bulb. Watch for the first sign of movement as the crystal melts.

Pure liquids: This technique, using an inverted capillary or melting point tube, sealed at the top, can measure the boiling point of samples of 1ml. Try distilled water, ethanol (B.P. 78°C). Adding salt to distilled water increases the boiling point.

How to purify a solid: Use salt mixed with some sand and a little litmus solution to colour it. Use about 10g per group. After adding water and stirring, add 1 spatula of fine charcoal powder, stir and warm to absorb the litmus dye. Filter, evaporate. Assess the success by comparison with the original uncontaminated salt. The melting point for sodium chloride is about 800°C, obviously impractical for pupils to test.

Separating soluble mixtures by chromatography: Emphasise that with the ascending paper chromatography, the start line (if used) must be in pencil not ink, that small samples work best and that the sample must be above the solvent level at the start.

For silver nitrate solution (dilute 0.05 - 0.1M), wait until the solvent front has almost reached to the top of the paper strip, remove it and immerse it in a solution of potassium chromate. This produces a reddish spot as the silver nitrate reacts (silver chromate). Carefully rinse the paper strip in running water and dry with a hair dryer. This shows that 'invisible' materials can be chromatographed as well.

Squish the squash thief: The rule is that, under the same conditions, the same component will travel the same distance. The thief was drinking the secret formula.

Acids and alkalis (page 16)
Warn about the dangers associated with acids and alkalis and the necessity to flood with water if any of the material is splashed on to the skin. Safety glasses are essential.

Indicator paper tests: Wide-range pH paper is best. One way is to issue each pupil with 6 x 1cm pieces to test materials at home, and collate the results later. They should be aware of the importance of water, for example by testing dry citric acid crystals and then adding water.

pHew! (page 17)
To see all the universal indicator colours, place water + indicator + enough hydrochloric acid to turn it red, in a conical flask. Add dilute ammonia solution, with shaking, from a burette or dropper.

Acid and alkali reactions (pages 17-19)
A pinch of salt: Discuss the necessity of carrying out the experiment twice, the second time without indicator to avoid producing a contaminated sample of the salt. Try alternative methods of evaporation, eg: window sill, oven, waterbath. Compare crystal sizes. Try a few drops on a microscope slide, evaporate the water and examine.

Give plenty of opportunities to discuss and try out the general word equations for neutralisation.

Discuss bases/alkalis to clarify the issue: all alkalis are bases, some bases are alkalis (soluble ones).

Experiment: Pupils will probably recognise the salt as copper sulphate.

The card method is generally successful in conveying the meaning of symbol equations, although examples must be chosen carefully to avoid early problems with balancing the equations.

Acid rain (page 19)

Clearly this is a much simplified account. Extend by discussing the acidic carbon dioxide that forms carbonic acid in rain and the nitrogen oxides from car exhausts and elsewhere that give nitric acid. Discuss the increasing importance of this problem since the Industrial Revolution, and why it has occurred.

Speeding along (pages 19-20)

Use dilute 2M hydrochloric acid and widely separated temperatures. The reasons for the time differences need to be discussed - more energy, faster rate.

Concentrations: Place the acid in a burette to speed up the measuring out at the start. Ask pupils why the total volume must be constant, in terms of fair tests. The stronger the acid, the faster the reaction or the less the time needed to complete the reaction.

Thiosulphate experiment: Use dilute 2M hydrochloric acid and a solution of sodium thiosulphate of about 40g/litre. Emphasise that accurate measurements are essential. The pencil cross should be lightly drawn or it may never disappear. The total volume remains constant at 50ml. A precipitate of yellow sulphur forms and obscures the pencil cross. The gas produced is sulphur dioxide, so good ventilation is needed. The fastest reaction, Mixture E, takes about 1 minute.

Particle size: Discuss the idea of surface area, using a simple example like cutting a slab of butter to create new surfaces with the same mass in total.
Safety:
Safety glasses essential. Warn about the dangers of fast reaction, add the acid slowly.

Going nowhere fast (page 21)

Copper sulphate is not a catalyst since, although the reaction accelerates, the copper sulphate is converted to copper metal and cannot be recovered at the end.

Hydrogen peroxide: Use 20 volume strength solution. Carbon has no significant effect but both of the others catalyse the conversion to water + oxygen gas.

Too big for their own good (page 21)

Emphasise the unpredictability of radioactive decay, that there is no way of predicting when a particular atom will decay. Also make clear that radioactive decay cannot be changed by catalysts, temperature, etc.

Background radiation: Discuss the idea of 'safe levels' of radiation, whether there is such a thing or not, and the long time-scale of biological effects. The National Radiological Protection Board has identified thousands of houses where there is a potential risk from radon.

The NRPB advises about improved ventilation or sealing floors and walls to reduce any risk.

Extend, if a geiger counter is available, by measuring the local background radiation, taking several readings and comparing. Try the stopping power of various metals like lead and aluminium.

If radioactive sources are used, ensure that you follow the guidelines published by the DES: *Ionising radiations in educational establishments*.

Industrial uses include: irradiation of food; detection of leaks within pipes; detection of thickness of materials.

Nuclear power (page 22-23)
Free information is available from the nuclear industry, some in class sets. The potential for discussion is very great here, since much controversy surrounds the industry. Also, make it clear that such ideas as the 'greenhouse effect' are by no means universally accepted within the international community.

Raw materials (page 23)
This topic is best approached by class discussion and/or a library search, starting with some key references.

Problems, problems (page 24)
This is a very complex issue. For example, to build a new zinc mine the operator must prove enough zinc ore is present, to justify the capital cost. The geologists drill and prove that enough ore is available for 20 years, then they stop looking since this is long enough to make the mine an economic proposition. When the government asks what reserves the mine has, the answer is "20 years". The next day a newspaper says, "Zinc will run out in 20 years". This approach can be generalised to other raw materials.

The problems: These are obviously open-ended problems to which there can be no single solution. The important issues are the assessment of the evidence and the solutions that derive from this.

Materials Book 3 offers the following National Curriculum Assessment Opportunities:

Attainment Target	Level	SofA	Pages
AT5	6	c	24
	7	a	23,24
		b	24
	8		24
AT6	3	a	23
	4	d	1
		e	1,2
	5	b	16-20
		c	10,13-16
	6	a	10-13
		b	2,3,12
AT7	4	a	10,12,17,18
		b	23
	6	a	16-19
	7	a	19-21
AT8	4	a	1,2
	5	a	1-3,7,8
	6	a	1
		c	8,17,18
	7	a	1
		b	5,7-10
		c	3,6,10
		d	21-23
AT10	5	c	5
AT13	4	b	22,23
	5	a	23,24
		b	23,24
	7	c	23
	8	b	23,24
		c	22

COMMUNICATIONS BOOK 1
ELECTRICITY, MAGNETISM AND LIGHT

Circuit training (pages 2-3)

The work on circuits is intended as revision of Key Stage 2 work. Most pupils would be expected to complete this section with little difficulty, although a few may need help and extra exercises may be required. Work on series and parallel circuits is introduced on pages 18 and 19.

Page 3: The work on electrical symbols may be extended if desired.

Getting the push (pages 3-4)

The experiment in making a battery from a lemon or potato needs careful setting up. Clean the electrodes with emery paper. Ensure the electrodes are placed near each other and a low voltage bulb is used. Ask the pupils questions to check their understanding of the production of electrical energy from the chemical reaction taking place within the fruit. This discussion should naturally lead on to the principle of the electric cell and the dry cell.

Voltmeter: Demonstrate the function of this or use the exercise as a means of assessment. The positioning of the meter into the circuit will need further explanantion. The use of a voltmeter should be encouraged more than once, so that pupils become confident in its use.

Current accounts (pages 4-5)

Ammeter: As with the voltmeter, demonstrate the function of the ammeter, or use the exercise for assessment purposes. Explain carefully the positioning of the ammeter into the circuit and encourage its use whenever the opportunity arises.

Testing conductors and insulators: It may be necessary to produce circuit boards ready set up for this exercise. Alternatively, it could be used as a revision of circuitry work. Try and select novel objects for testing, things to which the pupils would easily relate.

Effects of electrical current (page 5)

A selection of wires is required for this investigation. Wires to test could include copper, nichrome, aluminium, iron, etc. The procedure may be extended to another lesson, if necessary. As an extension, the pupils could be set the task of producing an 'electric fire element', light bulb 'filament' or 'immersion heater'. They should explain their procedure, why they selected the particular wire they did, why they selected the length, etc. What would happen if the wire was made longer/shorter?

Opposites attract (page 6)

This page presents an excellent opportunity for emphasising the dangers of electricity. See also pages 13-14.

Electrolysis: Time should be spent explaining the basics of electrolysis and its effects. The picture shows the set up for electrolysis but it may be necessary to extend this with verbal or further written information. The pupils may be allowed to test other liquids/solutions and to draw up a table of comparisons. This could then be used as a stimulus for further discussion.

Pupils could be given distilled water, told to add sodium chloride gradually and to note any effects observed. Similar experiments could be completed using distilled water and adding a) dilute acid and b) sucrose. Sucrose does not dissociate into ions, so no current flows.

Electrolysis (page 7)

The process of electroplating is explained as one aspect of electrolysis. The example given could be elaborated upon through a discussion of classic cars, 60's furniture, jewellery, bicycle parts, etc.

Charge! (page 8)

The comb and balloon activities could be extended to include a charged/uncharged gold leaf electroscope, etc. It may be possible to arange a circus of activities that would easily demonstrate the phenomenon.

Types of rod which can be used include polythene, acetate, glass and ebony. The Van der Graaff generator can provide a very popular and effective demonstration here, being used to demonstrate, among other things, repulsion of like charges and a 'lightning' effect.
Safety:
Pupils with any kind of heart condition should not be allowed to become charged using the generator.

Electromagnetism (pages 9-10)

It is possible to demonstrate the magnetic field around a wire using an OHP as the base. If the plotting compasses are transparent top and bottom, their images will be projected onto the screen. As the current is switched on, the needles are easily seen to move accordingly. Iron filings sprinkled on the card and gently tapped when the current is on, show the shape of the magnetic field well.

Discussing electromagnetism and its affects could pave the way for work on relays and miniature circuit breakers, earth leakage circuit breakers, etc (see pages 14 and 16).

Page 10: It is essential to have a very strong magnet for the generator activity if a deflection is to be demonstrated and observed by all pupils. Care should be taken in handling such a magnet. A light beam galvanometer gives a large deflection, and shows the direction of the current as the wire moves up and down. A demonstration meter with an ac milli-amp scale also works. If a strong magnet is not available, a reasonably strong bar magnet moved through a solenoid also works.

Dynamo: This could be demonstrated in class using the set up from the Nuffield Energy Kit. Pupils could also be encouraged to bring in their own bicycles, if they have a dynamo system fixed. Who can make the bulb glow the brightest? The ac output from a bicycle type dynamo can easily be displayed on a cathode ray oscilloscope.

At home with electricity (pages 10-11)

The work on electrical appliances could be linked with Humanities as a mini-project or investigation. It may be combined with a trip to a museum to underline the progress made in recent years in this area.

Getting it home (page 12)

This topic may need considerable input from the teacher. The information described in the pupil's book is easily demonstrated in the laboratory.

The dangers of playing near electrical substations and pylons should be emphasised.

The work on transformers in the home could be a homework or it could be used following a group discussion of the merits of transformers. Transformers from domestic appliances could be made available for the pupils to examine. Which appliance do they think benefited from each transformer?

Safety first (pages 13-15)

The work on safety offers another opportunity to draw out the relative merits of electricity. Emphasis should be placed on the usefulness of electricity when it is treated with respect and used correctly. The suggestion of producing posters could be extended into a project leading to a public display to which younger children from the feeder schools could be invited.

Consumer units: Pupils could be set the task of locating the consumer unit in their home and ascertaining its type.

A demonstration or class practical using a piece of steel wool as a fuse, shows what happens when a fuse blows.
Safety:
Quite a high current is needed and the wire gets very hot before you see it glow and melt.

Basic work on plug wiring could be introduced and may be extended by setting pupils the problem of ascertaining the difficulty of wiring a plug if the fingers are stiffened through arthritis. The finger joints could be taped over to simulate the complaint. As an extension to this, pupils could design a plug that would allow people with arthritis to wire it up without difficulty.

An exercise in replacing blown fuses could also be carried out.

Modern circuit breakers are becoming more widely known and time should be spent exploring the developments in this area.

Page 15: An exercise could be set for pupils to investigate the various appliances at home and check the fuses in the plugs.

Watts up? (pages 16-17)

Pupils will probably need help with meter readings and calculations. They could be asked to find out how much electricity is used in their homes in one week and the cost could then be calculated.

This work could coincide with a trip to the local electricity company.

Lighting circuits (pages 18-19)

Pupils may already have experience of parallel circuits from Key Stage 2, in which case this section can be used as a means of revision.

The exercise with the two-way switch could lead into information about other switching systems, including industrial switchgear.

The ring main: It may be possible in the laboratory to construct a working model of a ring main and/or a lighting circuit including a two-way switch for the stairs, using a low voltage circuit. This could be useful as a link with technology.

Lights up! (page 20)

As an extension to this topic, consider what can be clearly seen at different light levels. Set up objects of different colour and brightness in a lightproof box. The box can be a cardboard one with a lid which has a small pinhole. Paint the inside of the box black and use a low voltage bulb to provide the light. The brightness can be controlled using a rheostat. Observe the objects at different light levels and compare.

Seeing the light (page 21)

Pupils could investigate what is the best clothing to be worn at night. Various materials (matt, shiny, fluorescent, reflective) could be observed in darkness, then with light from a torch.

Shadow play (page 21)

The work on shadows can be extended to look at silhouette theatre, shadow plays, etc.

What happens to the size/definition of shadows when the light source is brighter/moved nearer or further?

Travelling light (page 22)

Pupils could also find out about eclipses of the sun and moon and link this with work on shadows and light travelling in straight lines.

Electromagnetic radiation (page 22)

The detection of various parts of the electromagnetic spectrum by other living things could be discussed here, especially the use of ultraviolet light by insects such as bees and butterflies, and the use of infra-red light by night hunters and some snakes.

Light work (pages 23-25)

Reflection: A good resource for work on reflection light is the flexible mirror, available from Griffin & George or Phillip Harris. Pupils could be issued with these for all the work mentioned in the text. They are especially useful for Activity 98. The idea of the normal needs to be introduced at some stage during or after the investigation on reflection.

As extension activities, pupils could build a working model of a periscope or set up an early warning system, using mirrors, to warn pupils of the approach of the teacher!

Refraction: A circus of practicals is possible here. A camera, microscope or projector could be examined to demonstrate the use of lenses in instruments. Pupils may be set the task of constructing a telescope, simple camera, etc.

Practical work may be done as a follow-up to consideration of the photograph at the top of page 25, using a glass or plastic block and a ray box with a single, fine beam of light. Place the block on paper in a darkened room and draw round it. Then observe and draw the incident and emergent beams. Connect the points at the interface of the air and block to show refraction.

A group activity which could be used as a follow-up, is the coin in the cup trick. Put a coin in a plastic cup, then move the head until the coin is just out of view. Fill the cup with water and the coin becomes visible.

Lenses: Pupils could be given a selection of converging lenses of different focal lengths (eg 10, 20 and 50cm) and asked to find out if the thickness of the lens affects how far the focus is from the lens.

The spectrum (page 26)

This practical can prove problematic with the incident and refracted beam paths. It is also more successful if the incident beam is focussed before entering the prism. Pupils may be set the problem of comparing focussed and unfocussed incident beams of light. The results and observations could form a basis for discussion.

Pupils who finish the activity quickly could be asked to try and recombine the separate colours into a single beam again.

Colours (pages 27-28)

Work on splitting light leads automatically on to mixing different colours of light. The traditional methods of Newton's disc and home-made spinners could play a part here as a support activity.

Work on primary and secondary colours and the colour triangle is a little difficult to organise, although very rewarding. It must be possible to control the light intensity of each light box in the set up described. It is unlikely that true secondary colours will be produced each time but there will certainly be a distinct change that all pupils should observe.

Page 28: Pupils seem to enjoy 'playing' with the light to see how many different colours they can produce.

As an extension, consider how a television can produce such a variety of colours when it has just three electron guns.

The production of colours by absorption is the function of gels. This may need a little explanation. Explain to pupils what happens if you line up a gel of red, blue and green one after the other in the path of a beam of light. As an extension to Question 122, consider why fire engines are red. Is red the best colour to be seen from a distance?

The eye (page 29)
Compare the eyes of different types of animal: snake or lizard; fish; bird; mammal.

Colour vision: There is no need to go into too much detail about the retina and the rods and cones. It may be better to concentrate on the 'everyday' aspects of colour vision, following on from the work at the end of page 28, eg: Do darker colours stand out well? How far away do we need to go before we cannot make out a given colour?

These exercises should lead pupils to realise that we all see slightly differently. What may appear normal to one is not to another. This could extend into work on perception.

The topic of colour blindness usually holds interest, especially if a member of the group has the defect. The use of the full Ishihara pack is useful in demonstrating differences in perception. A pupils with red/green deficiency is able to describe what they see, opening up some purposeful discussion. Why would it be difficult for such a person to be an electrician, telephone engineer, etc?

Seeing is believing (page 30)
The use of optical illusions may have been introduced at Key Stage 2. It is important to try to present novel images. Pupils may take on the challenge of producing their own illusions, although it is probably more difficult than they suppose. The 'bendy' pencil problem is an illusion which could lead on to the next section. Hold a pencil between thumb and index finger. Move your hand rapidly up and down as the pencil is observed.

Seeing double (page 30)
The discs are mounted on needles or thin dowel fixed into a firm base. The discs vary in size from 10mm to 50mm diameter, with an obvious difference between each. About 5 discs are required. The discs are set out in a line in front of the person being tested. Each one is set at a slightly different distance from the next. The bases are obscured by a board or rule. The person being tested should observe the discs through just one eye and try to determine which disc is nearest and which furthest away. They are then asked to judge using both eyes.

As an extension, do a similar investigation using peas spread onto the desk surface. The testee has to pick up the peas quickly between thumb and index finger only, while observing with just one eye.

Eye problems (pages 31-32)

The effects of long and short sight can be shown as follows: Fill a 5-litre round-bottomed flask with water and fluorescein dye. Support the flask in some way and fasten 'lenses' to the equator of the flask using Blu-Tack. The lenses have varying focal lengths to mimic the effects required, eg for short sight, the lens will have a focal length shorter than the diameter of the flask. Shine a high intensity light source at each of the lenses in turn and observe the cone of light.

This can be extended by placing the appropriate 'corrective' lens in front of the flask to show the effect of wearing spectacles or contact lenses.

Page 32: Extending eye defects to consideration of the plight of the blind person is not only scientific investigation, it also illustrates to pupils the importance of knowing your environment as well as possible. In addition, it raises the problem of providing adequate information.

Activity 136 could be used to make pupils far more aware of their surroundings, examining issues of texture, sound, smell, etc, and why colour is of no use in the circumstances. Discuss the attributes which could be used and then move around the immediate area describing it in the agreed terms. It may be possible to use pupils as examples of people who are blind and have them follow the instructions given.

This work also raises the issue of the importance of our other senses and that we should not neglect their development.

The work could include a visit from a blind person who lives locally, or a representative of the Royal National Institute for the Blind, who could explain the recent developments for the sight impaired.

This topic could be extended to discuss the blind spot which we all have (see the diagram on page 29). Pupils could find their own blind spot as follows. Draw a bold cross and a dot 6cm apart on paper. Hold the paper at arm's length. Close the left eye and concentrate on the cross with the right eye. *Slowly* bring the paper towards you. When the image of the dot falls on the blind spot, it will seem to disappear.

Communications Book 1 offers the following National Curriculum Assessment Opportunities:

Attainment Target	Level	SofA	Pages
AT11	Level 2	b	6,13,14
	Level 3	a	5,6
		b	1,18
	Level 4		2,18
	Level 5	a	2,3,18
		b	5,6
	Level 6	a	4
		b	8
		c	10 (in part),13,14
		d	16,17

Attainment Target	Level	SofA	Pages
AT11	Level 7	a	9 (in part),12(in part)
		b	6,7
AT15	Level 2	a	21
	Level 3	a	23,24,25
		b	23
	Level 4	a	21
		b	21,22
	Level 5		23
	Level 6	a	24- 25 (in part), 26
		b	29
		c	31,32
	Level 7	b	22
		c	22 (in part)
	Level 9	a	22 (in part)

COMMUNICATIONS BOOK 2

SOUND AND ELECTRONICS

At the recording studio (pages 1-3)

Page 2 : This page, and page 3, may be best approached by pupils working in groups. Each group could be asked to find out about a particular device. They could report back to the class in a variety of ways including posters, short talks, and using audio or video tape. If posters are chosen, then computers could be used to present the information in text, graph or graphic form. Companies such as BT are often very helpful in providing information relevant to their area.

Page 3: Most schools will not have access to multi-track recording machines but a comparison could be made between old mono and stereo recordings on tape or record.

Hello, Mr Chips (pages 4-6)

Page 4: Pupils could produce displays of the type of information we store as numbers, eg bar codes, post codes, prices, sizes, dates of birth. The class could pool various pieces of information such as their dates of birth. This would provide an opportunity to use a data base to display the information in tabular, graphical or pie chart form. The data base would need to have been set up in advance. The exercise could be extended by asking the pupils for selective information from the data base.

Pages 5-6: The different storage devices could be demonstrated from a selection of paper, discs, records, tape, etc. A simple short program could be typed into a computer, stored and run to demonstrate that computers respond to the instructions they are given. For example, this program in BBC Basic plots an envelope.

```
10 mode 1
20 for x=0 to 900 step 50
30 move x, 0
40 let y=900-x
50 draw 0,y
60 for i=0 to 200: next i
70 next x
80 end
```

Little wonders (pages 7-8)

Page 7: Pupils could look at some old chips to get the idea of exactly how small the components are and the idea that what actually takes up the room are the legs/ connections to other chips/devices. The input/process/output, etc could be related to other 'systems' such as a lesson where teacher = input, etc.

Page 8: This gives the pupils the opportunity to set up their own databases. Again group work could be useful here, given the constraints on access to computers which sometimes exist.

How alarming (pages 8-9)

Alarm circuits which respond to physical situations often contain sensors. Simple examples of these, such as light dependent resistors (LDR), thermistors, pressure pads and switches, could be examined in class. Simple series circuits could be built, involving LDRs or thermistors with lights, lights emitting diodes (LED), buzzers, etc as the alarm. Revision from Communications Book 1 may be needed before these circuits, and Activities 19 and 20, are tackled.

Logic gates (pages 10-13)

Pages 10-11: Truth tables not in the pupils book:

NOT	input	output		OR	inputs		ouput
	1	0			0	0	0
	0	1			1	0	1
					0	1	1
					1	1	1

Page 12:

NAND	inputs		output		NOR	inputs		output
	0	0	1			0	0	1
	1	0	1			1	0	0
	0	1	1			0	1	0
	1	1	0			1	1	0

Activity 27-28: Truth table at present, ie at least one window *and* the door must be open before the bell rings:

window 1	window 2	output of OR	door	final output
0	0	0	0	0
1	0	1	0	0
0	1	1	0	0
1	1	1	0	0
0	0	0	1	0
1	0	1	1	1
0	1	1	1	1
1	1	1	1	1

To correct the circuit, change the AND gate for an OR gate which will make the alarm ring when one window or the other, or the door, opens.

Activity 29: The circuit needed is as follows:

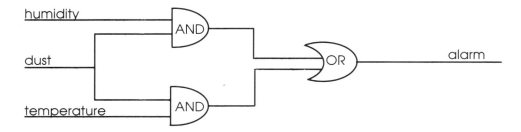

humidity	dust	temp	AND(h&d)	AND(d&t)	OR output
0	0	0	0	0	0
1	0	0	0	0	0
0	1	0	0	0	0
1	1	0	1	0	1
0	0	1	0	0	0
1	0	1	0	0	0
0	1	1	0	1	1
1	1	1	1	1	1

Digital and analogue signals (pages 13-15)

Page 13: Analogue and digital signals could be simulated on a cathode ray oscilloscope by showing sine and square wave functions from a signal generator. As well as watches, analogue and digital ammeters and/or voltmeters could be used. If the school has computer interfaced sensing equipment, the need for analogue to digital converters (ADC) could be discussed.

Pages 14-15: There are many methods of approaching the project pages, with many variables to consider. The approach may well be determined by the ability/size of the class, the type of equipment available in the school and the time available. Pupils could be encouraged to discuss their ideas in groups and to concentrate on one or more.

How sound is made (pages 17-18)

Page 17: There is plenty of opportunity here to experiment with different types of instrument (perhaps you could raid the music department!), Groups could make recordings of different instruments and ask the rest of the class to guess what was vibrating in each case. Vibrations which produce the voice can easily be felt if the fingertips are placed lightly on the throat. Activity 50 would make a good information search for homework or could alternatively be approached through one of the many excellent wildlife videos now available. The idea of vibrating air columns (Activity 51) can be demonstrated by inserting one end of an open-ended glass tube (diameter approximately 5 cm) into a cylinder of water and blowing across the top. As the tube is raised or lowered to alter the column length, the note is heard to change.

Page 18: Activity 52 may be extended to a discussion on tuning instruments and what can be changed to alter the pitch of various instruments (see also page 24). Activity 53 can also be completed as a demonstration by sitting the beaker on an OHP. The activity could be extended to find out whether the effect differs according to how hard a tuning fork is struck. If a sound/resonating box is used, the idea of louder sounds having increased energy can also be discussed.

Making waves (page 19)

Pulses sent down a slinky, demonstrate very well how sound travels. Both increased amplitude and frequency may be demonstrated. The cathode ray oscilloscope (CRO) could be introduced here (see also page 22), connected to a signal generator and loudspeaker to demonstrate what a sound wave 'looks' like and the effect of increasing amplitude and frequency. The idea of radio and LW/MW needs to be considered very carefully, or many pupils will have the idea that on LW radio the sound has a long wavelength, whereas it is the carrier wave which has the long wavelength.

The sounds of silence (page 20)

The hearing range of humans (20Hz-20KHz, with young people generally have better hearing than older people at the top of the range) can be demonstrated here using a CRO, signal generator and loudspeaker. If you can get hold of a dog whistle and use a microphone connected to a CRO, pupils can see that it does indeed produce a 'sound' even though we cannot hear it. This provides a good link to an information search, discussion or video on communication and ultrasound. Infrasound could also be included. The experiment involving a ringing bell in a bell jar attached to a vacuum pump, demonstrates the need for a medium in order for sound to travel.

The speed of sound (pages 20-21)

Alternative methods for measuring the speed of sound, if the school does not have sound switches, include timing the interval between a clap and its echo from a high building or wall, then using the equation *speed = distance/time.* Long metal railings may also be used. One pupil taps one end with a stick and starts a stopclock, which is stopped when another pupil at the other end signals they have heard the sound. The same equation may then be used. Note that this does not give the speed of sound in *air.*

Loudness (page 22)

This page allows pupils to investigate the CRO in greater depth. The screen can be described as a 'moving graph' whose scales are changed using the relevant dials on the front. Pupils can try making a variety of sounds using instruments, tuning forks with sound/ resonating boxes and their voices. Those who can whistle well can often produce very good traces on the screen.

Noise can annoy (page 23)

The sound meter could be introduced as another instrument for measuring sound levels. When discussing the decibel scale, it is important to remember that it is logarithmic and that an increase in level from 10dB to 20dB does not therefore mean the noise level has doubled. It has considerably more than doubled. Pupils could conduct their own noise survey in various places by recording exactly what they hear over a short period, eg 5 minutes.

Pitch (page 24)

Put small polystyrene balls on a cone speaker attached to a signal generator and observe what happens to them as the pitch/frequency changes.

The ear (page 25)

If available, videos and models are probably the best way to help pupils understand this topic fully.

SCIENCE THEMES

COMMUNICATIONS BOOK 2

Hearing tests (page 26)
The practicals involving hearing tests could be completed as explorations, providing pupils with opportunities to plan experiments, control variables, interpret results and ensure fair tests.

Hearing problems (page 26)
Some of the types of deafness could be discussed, along with a demonstration/discussion of how hearing aids work.

The microphone/The loudspeaker/The radio/The telephone (pages 27-28)
Ideally examples of microphones, loudspeakers, simple radios and the telephones should be taken to bits and looked at. Work should be linked to that completed previously on current and magnetic fields in Communications Book 1. If time is available, a simple radio could be built as extension work, linking this section with previous work done on circuits.

Information transmission systems (page 28)
Pupils could build their own model 'telegraph' system using switches and bulbs or buzzers and use it to send messages. Morse code (although now outdated with modern communications equipment) is the obvious way of sending the messages.

The relay (page 29)
If the school has a demonstration relay, the mechanism can be looked at in detail. Again, this work should be linked to work completed in Communications Book 1.

On the rebound/Sound insulation (page 29)
Pupils could investigate how different surfaces deaden sound. A small transistor or speaker is placed inside a box. The box is lined with various materials in turn, eg bubble wrap, egg boxes, felt material, foam material, silver foil, etc to see which deadens the sound most effectively.

Communications Book 2 offers the following National Curriculum Assessment Opportunities:

Attainment Target	Level	SofA	Pages
AT11	Level 6	c	29
AT12	Level 1		2
	Level 2	a	2
		b	4-7
	Level 3	a	2,6-8
		b	3-5,8,30,31
		c	8
	Level 4	a	2,7,9,14,15
		b	9
	Level 5	a	10-11(in part), 14-15(in part), 29(in part)
		b	10-12
	Level 6	a	13
		b	27,28,30,31
	Level 7	a	27,28,30,31
AT14	Level 1		17
	Level 2	b	17
	Level 3	a	17(in part), 18
		b	18,19
	Level 4		20,21
	Level 5	a	19,24
		b	22
		c	23
	Level 6	a	18
		b	25,26
		c	27,28
	Level 7		28,30,31

SOME IDEAS TO TEST (page 3)

The notes below also apply to page 30 of the pupil's book. The two topics are similar in approach and the notes therefore apply equally well to both.

Pupils discuss a number of statements/hypotheses and decide whether they are reasonable or not. They then devise fair tests that will help them to discover if the idea is 'true' or not.

BACKGROUND INFORMATION AND WAYS FORWARD

The main aim is to provoke discussion and to make pupils aware that the nature of science is such that people develop ideas and then use a logical process in deciding whether these ideas are reasonable or not. The exercise will thus introduce pupils to the idea of hypotheses, although they do not need to know the actual word. The difference between good and poor science depends on the extent/rigour to which the ideas are tested. Of course not all ideas are directly testable and pupils can discover this through this topic.

People have many beliefs about the world. There is a danger that ideas can be too readily accepted without sufficient supporting evidence. Many ideas/beliefs are really myths, rather than what we might consider to be fact.

Pupils should examine the statements and decide whether they are testable or not. They should discover that to make ideas testable they may need to rephrase them. Pupils will profit by doing this exercise in small groups and much discussion/debate should be encouraged.

Some of the ideas might well be used to develop projects or explorations. However, pupils should recognise the difference between an open-ended statement and one that is stated simply and precisely enough to permit an answer of 'yes' or 'no'.

Pupils could also be made aware of 'the tentative nature of proof', ie just because a particular result is obtained, does it necessarily mean that it will always be obtained given that set of circumstances (will a coin always land head or tails)?

Once groups have produced some fair tests, they could be exchanged with those of other groups to enable further discussion/debate.

Ideally this topic is a class exercise, although it could be offered as homework. However, pupils could be asked to develop more ideas for homework, for example to make a list of superstitions and then to treat them in a similar way.

There is clearly some overlap here with aspects of Attainment Target 1 but no apology is made since pupils should discover that ideas such as these are in the very nature of science!

NATIONAL CURRICULUM ASSESSMENT OPPORTUNITIES

AT17   Level 5   SofA   a,b

AT1   Level 3   SofA   a
         Level 4   SofA   a,b,c,d

MARIE CURIE (page 4)

The discovery of radium by Marie Curie is briefly described. A simple description of radioactivity is given. Pupils are then invited to consider radioactive materials in terms of their uses and of safety.

BACKGROUND INFORMATION AND WAYS FORWARD

This topic is an example of how scientific knowledge evolves, ie one person's discoveries usually follow directly from another's. Pierre Curie is included to illustrate the usefulness and importance of teamwork in science. Henri Becquerel discovered radioactivity when he found that uranium salts extracted from the mineral pitchblende clouded photographic plates. (This is a good example of a scientific 'accident' and of the great importance of observation skills!) Pitchblende is a blackish rock.

Marie Curie's special contribution here was in recognising that there might be further radioactive substances - and in her great chemical skills in extraction and purification. She showed great perseverance, working in poor conditions (a leaky old shed) over many months, culminating in the isolation of radium and polonium. She was awarded *two* Nobel prizes (in physics and chemistry). Her daughter Irene Joliot-Curie also received a Nobel prize for her work on radioactivity.

The visible glow that is implied is a reaction between the ionising radiation and the oxygen in the air. Not all radioactive substances give a visible glow.

Several tonnes of pitchblende yielded only 100 milligrams of radium. It is this fact which should suggest to the pupils that radium is rare.

Pupils should be encouraged to discuss and say what they know of radioactivity. They could be asked to find out its uses. At this stage their findings will probably be limited to nuclear energy and electricity, nuclear bombs/missiles and the pollution problems. They should be able to discover that radioactive substances can cause various cancers but should equally learn that these substances can also be used to treat certain cancers. It would also be useful to spend some time on the use of X-rays, perhaps as an introduction to skeletons and other internal organs. One profitable exercise is for pupils to carry out a survey of what other people (especially adults) know and think about radioactivity.

Pupils should be able to conclude that radioactive substances can be kept safely in lead and/or concrete containers. Of course there are different types of ionising radiation, and in fact some types will not even pass through paper!

This topic could serve as a useful introduction to separating techniques and to the idea of mixtures and compounds.

NATIONAL CURRICULUM ASSESSMENT OPPORTUNITIES

AT17	Level 4			AT6	Level 5	SofA	b
	Level 6	SofA	b		Level 6	SofA	b
	Level 7	SofA	a	AT7	Level 5	SofA	a
				AT8	Level 7	SofA	d

THINGS ARE NOT ALWAYS WHAT THEY SEEM (page 5)

The notes below also apply to page 19 of the pupil's book. The two topics are similar in approach.

Pupils are given examples of, and asked to consider, how observations can be misinterpreted.

BACKGROUND INFORMATION AND WAYS FORWARD

It is important that pupils understand that it is possible to be fooled by our senses and experiences. When we meet something that is novel to our experience we try to explain it by comparing it with our previous experiences. It was easy to misinterpret the lines on Mars as canals, since the only experience of such long 'structures' was the man-made equivalents on earth. Also (which is a greater problem) many people wanted to believe that life existed elsewhere. Similar misinterpretations resulted in the naming of certain parts of the Moon and Mars as seas.

The case of the Piltdown Man is probably the most famous of scientific hoaxes. The problem was that much of the scientific community believed that human beings evolved from the apes and was constantly searching for the missing link - fossil evidence of bones that were half ape/half human. It proved relatively easy to fool the scientists (in 1912). They were presented with a human skull with a jaw that was apelike. The evidence was accepted, until in 1953 it was shown that the bones had been modified to make them fit together. It would be better if scientists were not always so convinced that their theories are absolutely perfect!

Unfortunately, over the years, there has been a number of instances where scientists have falsified their results in the attempt to prove a theory. Once exposed, these people have become the focus of much humiliation and shame. Indeed one scientist committed suicide as a result. The point is that most scientific observations are shared between scientists and consequently truth and honesty are very highly valued. It is important that pupils approach this topic through discussion and learn to record results and observations accurately and honestly. The idea of getting a wrong result should not be met with guilt! The meaning/interpretation of results, whilst extremely important, is secondary to the presentation of accurate ones. Poor interpretations can always be improved upon, whereas results cannot always be re-obtained. Enquiries of teachers' cheating experiences should be handled with some tact, since we should seek to avoid setting bad examples.

Note that the man in picture E is moving a canal barge through a tunnel.

This topic could link with Earth in Space, evolution and possibly with some aspects of PSE.

NATIONAL CURRICULUM ASSESSMENT OPPORTUNITIES

AT17   Level 5   SofA   b

AT1   Level 3   SofA   f,g,
       Level 4   SofA   h,i
       Level 5   SofA   d

AT4   Level 3
AT16   Level 4   SofA   b

THOMAS EDISON (page 6)

A very brief account is given of Edison, making mention of his phonograph and light bulb. Pupils are asked to consider ways in which sound can be recorded, and to think about the impact the invention of the light bulb had on society.

BACKGROUND INFORMATION AND WAYS FORWARD

Edison is particularly famed for his prodigious inventiveness. He is an excellent example of the scientist as observer and problem solver. One of his early inventions was a machine for transmitting Morse code. It involved a drum on which the dots and dashes were recorded; when the drum was moved, these caused a needle to vibrate.

He noticed that loud noises also made the needle vibrate and it was this observation that led him to develop the phonograph. The first phonograph had the sound recorded on tin-foil rather than wax. The first recorded speech is of Edison reciting, "Mary had a little lamb...". Apparently, it was the first thing that came into his mind! Given short notice, what would the pupils say in such circumstances?

Edison was aware of the arc lamp, but it was considered expensive to use. His first successful bulb (incandescent lamp) had a filament made of cotton coated with carbon. It was sealed in a bulb with the air removed so that it did not burn up. Most modern light bulbs contain an inert gas which also glows when it is hot.

Pupils may need to find out what 'inert' means. This topic as presented could be a useful homework exercise. However, it could be extended to explore the relationships between sound vibrations, amplitude, frequency, pitch and volume. A paper cone with a pin put through the narrow end can be used to produce sound from a revolving record.

Vibrating rulers can be investigated, as can tuning forks vibrating in air and water.

Alternatively, pupils might like to consider and examine a variety of light sources, eg: torch bulbs, domestic light bulbs, fluorescent lamps, fire, candles, luminous paint, camping gas lamps (with mantle), etc.

NATIONAL CURRICULUM ASSESSMENT OPPORTUNITIES

AT17 Level 4

AT12 Level 3 SofA b
AT14 Level 3 SofA a,b
      Level 5 SofA a,b

WHERE DO DAISIES GROW? (page 7)

Pupils are asked to examine a series of photographs to decide where daisies grow best. They should then be allowed to find out for themselves. Having decided where they grow best, pupils "hypothesise", plan and carry out an investigation to find out why.

BACKGROUND INFORMATION AND WAYS FORWARD

Daisies are not particularly good photosynthesisers in that they need a lot of light. They only grow well in grass that is cut frequently.

Pupils should be encouraged to quantify numbers of daisies rather than just look. A fair test might include the use of quadrats and some form of random sampling. (Two metre sticks to form two edges of a quadrat would be sufficient.) The results are likely to be quite conclusive. In fact, daisies are so dependent on good light, that doing the starch test on a daisy from short grass and one from long grass will give distinctly different results!

Many daisies may seem not to be in flower, especially on recently cut grass. It is best not to count flowers, but whole plants; the leaves grow in rosettes. Pupils can easily learn how to identify them by observing a plant in flower first.

A successful investigation is likely to involve setting light as a variable, ie covering one plant whilst cutting grass and exposing another, then doing the starch test on each one. However, it is more important that the pupils' *own* ideas are tested.

The main aim of this topic is to encourage teamwork and collaboration. Pupils will find the task clear cut and should have a good idea of how to go about it.

NATIONAL CURRICULUM ASSESSMENT OPPORTUNITIES

AT17   Level 5   SofA   a,b

AT1   Level 3   SofA   a,c,f,h,i
       Level 4   SofA   a,b,c,d,h,i,j
AT2   Level 5   SofA   a
AT3   Level 6   SofA   b

MAGGOTS (pages 7-9)

Pupils are taken through an account of Francesco Redi's experiments which disproved the widely-held belief in spontaneous generation. The topic ends with an introduction to the life cycles of insects.

BACKGROUND INFORMATION AND WAYS FORWARD

This topic highlights how some beliefs are held without any hard evidence to support them. It emphasises the importance of good accurate observation and the need for a logical approach. The methods may seem similar to Pasteur's, but pupils should not confuse the generation of maggots with that of microbes. Nevertheless, the decaying of meat is largely the result of microbial action.

The topic is mainly a reading/discussion/pencil and paper exercise, and as such may prove difficult for some. However, pupils could adopt a practical approach, or it could be presented as a demonstration.

It is important that pupils work through the topic in small groups. There would be some profit in a mixed ability approach.

Pupils should be encouraged to do the questions one at a time. It should be noted that the more alert may find answers by reading ahead!

The mental exercise here is more important than getting a 'particular' correct answer.

NATIONAL CURRICULUM ASSESSMENT OPPORTUNITIES

AT17 Level 4
      Level 5   SofA   a,b
      Level 6   SofA   b
      Level 7   SofA   a

AT1   Level 3   SofA   a,c
      Level 4   SofA   a,b,c,d,i
      Level 5   SofA   a
AT2   Level 4   SofA   b

FLYING SHEEP (page 9)

Pupils are given a very brief account of the Montgolfier hot-air balloon. They then try to demonstrate that hot air rises and consider some consequences of the development.

BACKGROUND INFORMATION AND WAYS FORWARD

The Montgolfier brothers' early experiments were with small spheres under which they burnt straw.

Professor Charles gave the first public demonstration with a large hydrogen-filled balloon. However, it was the Montgolfiers who gave the first public demonstration carrying passengers - albeit a sheep, a cock and a duck. It would be worth asking the pupils why such animals were used!

The first manned flight took place in 1783 in a Montgolfier balloon. The simplest hot-air balloons can be made by setting light to the slightly closed opening of paper bags - an outdoor activity! More sophisticated ones can be made, although the balloon needs to be large enough to counteract any weight of a 'carried' fuel source.

Hot air rising can also be demonstrated simply by observing smoke, or more interestingly by suspending paper windmills above hot objects.

NATIONAL CURRICULUM ASSESSMENT OPPORTUNITIES

AT17   Level 4

AT1   Level 3   SofA   i
       Level 4   SofA   g,i,j
AT6   Level 5   SofA   a
       Level 6   SofA   e

WOMEN IN SCIENCE (page 10)

A short stimulus is given to raise the pupils' awareness of issues regarding women in science. It is followed by a series of tasks which involve survey and discussion, with pupils investigating differing attitudes to and expectations of science for boys and girls.

BACKGROUND INFORMATION AND WAYS FORWARD

It is difficult to identify any specific Statements of Attainment which relate to this topic! However, it is considered to be an important issue and very much part of the nature of science.

It was the author's aim to include more topics which gave account of women scientists. In fact, it proved most difficult to identify women scientists, particularly within the constraints of Key Stage 3. Remarkably few science texts at any level give credit to women. Indeed, few students of science (including teachers) are given factual information in this area.

It is hoped that the topic will engender much debate amongst the pupils. Teachers should give examples wherever possible of female pupils, past and present, that they know have been successful in their science studies, especially those who have followed careers in science and technology. It should be made clear that industry does require more women in this field and that there is now, in fact, some positive discrimination in favour of women.

It could be pointed out that in some societies, in particular the Soviet Union and China, women do play an active role in what we consider to be male-dominated careers.

SAVING ENERGY (page 11)

Pupils are presented with some reasons for needing energy, some sources of energy, and some problems associated with energy usage. They are then given a series of tasks relating to these, which look at energy conservation and pollution problems.

BACKGROUND INFORMATION AND WAYS FORWARD

The issues raised in this topic are fairly familiar but nevertheless relevant and important.

The topic could be used as a 'one-off' lesson or as a homework exercise. However, it contains much stimulus material and could form the basis of an exploration or project. Whichever approach is taken, pupils should be encouraged to discuss/debate the issues.

Pupils could investigate the ways in which buildings are insulated. They could design 'tests' to determine how effective these ways are. They could investigate the relative costs of insulating procedures and of heating and lighting different areas. They could investigate the impact of the motor car on the environment.

There are several energy sources in addition to those mentioned, eg: nuclear, wind, wave, solar, hydroelectric, burning refuse, etc. Pupils could explore the advantages and disadvantages of these. They could investigate the problems of carbon dioxide emissions and the greenhouse effect (see page 21 of their books). They could be asked to investigate the usage of bottles, tins and paper in their homes, the need for them, and what they do with them when they are no longer required.

NATIONAL CURRICULUM ASSESSMENT OPPORTUNITIES

AT17	Level 5	SofA	a,b
AT5	Level 4		
	Level 5	SofA	a
	Level 6	SofA	c
	Level 7	SofA	a,b
AT13	Level 3	SofA	a
	Level 4	SofA	a,b,c
	Level 5	SofA	a,b
	Level 6	SofA	a,d
	Level 7	SofA	c

THE WAY THINGS MOVE (page 12)

Pupils observe a cartoon diagram of the trajectories of various cannon balls. The diagram is accompanied by comments of early scientists. Pupils are then asked to decide which is the correct trajectory and to design and carry out a test to see if they are correct.

BACKGROUND INFORMATION AND WAYS FORWARD

Early scientists and philosophers believed that things were either celestial or earthly and that objects always fell to earth vertically. The only force that could alter the path of a falling object was celestial. Consequently, even though many observed that this was not the case, none dared disprove it. Even Leonardo da Vinci, who dared suggest the 'truth', did not try to demonstrate it.

Such knowledge becomes essential if an army wants its cannon balls to land on target. If the high point of the trajectory is above the target, then obviously the cannon ball will go too far.

Pupils should enjoy testing this idea. Their main problem will be applying the same force each time and actually observing the trajectory. They should be able to resolve the latter problem, though a reliable method might include the use of a video camera. Pupils should appreciate that the task is short enough to enable them to check their results several times.

Task 4 might be used as an extension exercise.

The knowledge gained from this should be useful to pupils to enable their 'shot', cricket ball, javelin, etc to go the furthest with the least force put into it.

NATIONAL CURRICULUM ASSESSMENT OPPORTUNITIES

```
AT17  Level 4
      Level 5   SofA   a,b
      Level 6   SofA   b
      Level 7   SofA   a

AT1   Level 3   SofA   a,b,c,e,f,i
      Level 4   SofA   b,c,d,e,g,h,i,j
      Level 5   SofA   a
AT10  Level 3   SofA   a
      Level 4   SofA   a,b,c,d
      Level 5   SofA   c
AT13  Level 3   SofA   c
```

MARCONI (page 13)

Pupils are given a very brief account of Marconi and his wireless transmitter. They are then asked to decipher and make up Morse code messages and to consider the impact of radio on society.

BACKGROUND INFORMATION AND WAYS FORWARD

Radio waves were discovered by Heinrich Hertz, but it was Marconi who was able to develop the idea and invent the wireless transmitter. Marconi was an Italian who was largely sponsored by Britain, where he carried out his research. His transmitter was used for sending Morse code signals. He gave several demonstrations over a period of two years and in each one he was able to transmit over a greater distance. It was in 1901 that he first arranged the successful transmission from Poldhu in Cornwall to a wooden hut near St. John's, Newfoundland.

Marconi's discoveries soon led to the invention of the 'modern' radio and the broadcast of voice, although he did not actually invent it himself. His work then led to the development of the radio, radar, television and, of course, all the other things that these made possible. The list is almost endless: from remote control of models/toys to satellite observations, communication with people on the moon, weather forecasting by radar, and so on. Marconi received the Nobel prize for Physics in 1909.

This topic can be further reinforced if pupils are allowed to build electrical circuits which include buzzers. The switch and buzzer could be in separate rooms connected by wire.

You may have facilities for building a simple radio receiver (these can usually be made inside one lesson).

An entertaining challenge is to equip pupils with only torches and sets of mirrors and to ask them to get a simple message from one room to another!

NOTE: The message reads, "Ask your teacher for extra homework".

NATIONAL CURRICULUM ASSESSMENT OPPORTUNITIES

AT17	Level 4			AT12	Level 4	SofA	a
					Level 6	SofA	b
AT11	Level 3	SofA	b		Level 7	SofA	b
	Level 4			AT14	Level 6	SofA	c
					Level 7		

PURE LIGHT (page 14)

Pupils are introduced to Einstein as a theoretical physicist. A simple explanation of the difference between ordinary and laser light is given. Pupils are then asked to design a set-up which delivers thin beams of light. Finally, pupils are asked to consider the use of lasers.

BACKGROUND INFORMATION AND WAYS FORWARD

Ordinary light is a mixture of light of different wavelengths. Each of these wavelengths (colours) behaves differently. The result is that ordinary light spreads out (radiates in all directions) and the individual 'particles' (photons) arrive at the target/observer at different times. However, laser light is extremely concentrated and made up of only one wavelength. The beam is parallel and the photons all hit the target at the same time. The most common laser is the ruby laser. Intense 'ordinary light' is first directed into it. The light is then reflected back and forth in the rod which stimulates atoms in the rod to emit even more light. When the light is intense enough it emerges from one end of the ruby rod. Impure light is scattered sideways out from one end of the rod leaving only the pure light to be emitted at the end. (It should be understood that the process is much more complex than this and will not be further explained here.) Note that the diagram implies that the laser beam is 'pulsed'. In this form it is much more powerful than if it were continuous.

Pupils are asked why Einstein did not build the laser. This is an important aspect when considering the nature of science. Many good ideas cannot be further developed until other technologies have become available. It might be worth asking pupils to consider examples of this in the form of: "What had to be invented before so and so could be invented?" If pupils succeed in making a beam of thin light, it might prove useful to substitute the apparatus for ray boxes in other light investigations.

Note also that if your department has a laser, its beam could be compared with that from their apparatus or a ray box, when it would be apparent that even their thin beam of light rapidly becomes wider. The use of lasers is rapidly becoming most extensive. Some examples are: in surgery, as a substitute for scalpels for the repair of retinas; in the military, for target finding, ranging; and in communications, for Hi Fi (CD players), video discs and the production of holograms.

SAFETY
You should not attempt to use laser equipment unless you have been properly instructed in its use and have been made aware of its safe handling.

NATIONAL CURRICULUM ASSESSMENT OPPORTUNITIES

AT17 Level 4
    Level 5 SofA a
    Level 6 SofA a,b

AT1 Level 4 SofA a,g,j
AT15 Level 3 SofA a
    Level 4 SofA b
    Level 7 SofA a,b

THE NATURE OF SCIENCE

PRESSURE POINTS (page 15)

Pupils are given a simple explanation of air pressure; how the mercury barometer works and how Pascal 'proved' that air pressure changes with altitude. The pupils then attempt various tasks which demonstrate air pressure and that air has weight.

NOTE: There is an error in the pupil's book. The air pressure shown at the top of the mountain should be 580mm and that at the bottom should be 660mm. This will be corrected in the first reprinting of the book.

BACKGROUND INFORMATION AND WAYS FORWARD

When a tube is filled with mercury and then inverted in a bowl of mercury, as in the diagram, the mercury falls a little from the top as a result of its weight. The space left at the top is a vacuum, the idea of which was difficult to accept in Torricelli's time. It was ungodly to think that 'nothing' could exist. However, it was Torricelli who was able to demonstrate that air had weight and that it pushed down on the mercury in the bowl and kept the mercury in the tube. It was Pascal who demonstrated that air pressure changes with altitude. As one moves up a mountain there is less air pushing down and therefore less air pressure; consequently, the mercury level is lower.

There is a weight difference between a full and an empty balloon, but an accurate top pan balance will be needed. It might prove easier to use a simple lever balance and suspend an inflated balloon from each end. Putting a piece of sellotape on one and piercing it with a pin will allow the air to escape slowly, allowing the heavy end to fall. Inverting a tumbler, with paper covering it, works well providing the tumbler is absolutely full and no air is allowed to enter whilst it is being inverted. A water barometer works well but its much greater length makes it inconvenient to use.

Air pressure is lower at any higher altitude and is zero in space. Hence there is no air pressure to keep the mercury in; indeed the mercury would have no weight. Air pressure is also lower in suction pumps and in the cabins of high altitude aircraft; this reduces the tendency to burst. Air pressure is higher at any lower altitude, including caves and in submarines (to stop them imploding). Air pressure is high on bright sunny days and lower on dull cloudy days. The modern altitude barometer (altimeter) is the anaeroid barometer which is compact and does not use mercury.

It might prove useful for pupils to find out atmospheric pressures daily and to relate these to weather changes. The topic could also link with other investigations concerned with vacuums, eg lack of sound transmission in vacuums; also with other studies concerning the nature of pressure.

NATIONAL CURRICULUM ASSESSMENT OPPORTUNITIES

AT17	Level 4			AT6	Level 4	SofA	c
	Level 5	SofA	a		Level 5	Sofa	a
	Level 6	SofA	a,b	AT9	Level 3	SofA	b,e
	Level 7	SofA	a		Level 7	SofA	a
				AT10	Level 4	SofA	c
AT1	Level 3	SofA	f,h,i		Level 6	SofA	b
	Level 4	SofA	h,i,j	AT13	Level 4	SofA	e
					Level 3	SofA	a

LOUIS PASTEUR (pages 16-17)

Pupils are presented with 'news' items of the period regarding disease, food spoilage and Pasteur's work. They are then asked to identify the problems and their causes.

BACKGROUND INFORMATION AND WAYS FORWARD

In spite of Redi's work, people did not understand why foods went bad or what caused diseases, even though by now microorganisms (bacteria) had been observed in bad foods and diseased animals. The idea of spontaneous generation was still held, ie that microbes came from decaying meat rather than causing it.

Pasteur was able finally to 'prove' that the microbes came from the air that was in contact with food. He did this by filtering air through gun-cotton and observing the trapped microbes with a microscope. He also showed that broth (nowadays nutrient broth) did not go cloudy and bad when in contact with filtered air but did with ordinary air. His most famous experiment involved putting some broth into a glass flask, the top of which was pulled out into a long thin S-shaped tube as in the picture on page 17. After heating the contents, he showed that it stayed clear for many months. His conclusion was that the dust carrying bacteria could not get round the S-bend. He realised that the bacteria in the air (and already in milk) caused the souring of milk. He was able to preserve milk by first heating it to destroy microbes and then sealing it.

Similarly, though it was known that yeast was needed to make wine and beer, he realised that it was airborne bacteria and dirty containers that caused wine and beer to turn into vinegar. Once most diseases were known to be caused by bacteria, it became obvious how the cows were getting anthrax. As a result, diseased animals were burned and surviving animals grazed on clean pastures.

As presented, this topic might prove difficult and the pupils would profit from some practical experience. Standard investigations might include heating and/or chilling milk and sealing it from the air. A fair test would involve leaving a sample unheated and open to the air. Another is the use of nutrient broth in sterilised test tubes. One could be left open, another covered with foil, another plugged with cotton wool, and another fitted with an S-tube. The broths should be sterilised and be bright and clear to start with.

The topic could serve as an introduction to disease and/or food preservation. Pupils should appreciate that there are more types of good/useful microbes than there are harmful ones.

SAFETY

You should not attempt to grow or examine bacteria until you are familiar with the appropriate aseptic techniques. However, the milk investigations are harmless.

NATIONAL CURRICULUM ASSESSMENT OPPORTUNITIES

AT17	Level 4				AT1	Level 3	SofA	a,b,c,h,i
	Level 5	SofA	a,b			Level 4	SofA	a,b,c,d,g,i,j
	Level 6	SofA	b		AT2	Level 4	SofA	b
	Level 7	SofA	a		AT3	Level 5	SofA	d

AT THE CENTRE OF THINGS (page 18)

Pupils are given a pre-Copernican view of the universe (Earth-centred) followed by the Copernican view (Sun-centred solar system), subsequently substantiated by Galileo's observations of the moons of Jupiter.

BACKGROUND INFORMATION AND WAYS FORWARD

The history of scientific thought, calculation and observation of the universe is vast. Only a simplistic account can be offered here. Most early theories of planetary movements were derived from mathematical thought, often in the attempt to confirm current beliefs rather than to account for observations. Essentially, the belief was that the Earth was at the centre of all things and that the planets and the Sun orbited around it. All this was then enclosed by a shell of stars. The shell was believed to be finite and nothing existed beyond it, ie the universe was limited. Such a belief allowed heaven to be placed in the shell - meaning that the Creator could be separate from the created (which was where 'he' would want to be).

Copernicus, by means of accurate observations and calculation, was able to demonstrate that the Earth was by no means at the centre and that the planets actually orbited the Sun. He made it clear that all bodies were in constant motion, including the Sun. Further, he maintained that the universe was infinite and that the stars were at varying distances. This was a most unpopular idea, particularly because it made the location of heaven impossible. Copernicus' work was consequently banned, but not before others had taken a grasp of his ideas.

One argument against his theory was that, if the Earth was moving, why did the Moon always stay with it? No one had any concept of the nature of gravity or that, beyond the atmosphere, nothingness or a vacuum did exist. This made it impossible for them to understand why the atmosphere did not blow away.

Pupils should be allowed to debate/discuss the issues involved in this topic. Perhaps there is room for role-play here. Pupils should find the information about orbits for themselves by data search. They could also endeavour to produce models to represent orbits and/or the solar system. Aspects of optics could be investigated and a telescope could be built.

The topic should prove useful as an introduction to further work on the nature of gravity and other forces, and to studies of Earth in space.

NATIONAL CURRICULUM ASSESSMENT OPPORTUNITIES

AT17	Level 4			AT10	Level 4	SofA	c
	Level 5	SofA	b	AT15	Level 6	SofA	a
	Level 6	SofA	b	AT16	Level 4	SofA	b,c
	Level 7				Level 6		
					Level 7	SofA	b
AT6	Level 5	SofA	a				

SEEING WHAT WE WANT TO SEE (page 19)

The notes below also apply to page 5 of the pupil's book. The two topics are similar in approach.

Pupils are given examples of, and asked to consider, how observations can be misinterpreted.

BACKGROUND INFORMATION AND WAYS FORWARD

It is important that pupils understand that it is possible to be fooled by our senses and experiences. When we meet something that is novel to our experience we try to explain it by comparing it with our previous experiences. It was easy to misinterpret the lines on Mars as canals, since the only experience of such long 'structures' was the man-made equivalents on earth. Also (which is a greater problem) many people wanted to believe that life existed elsewhere. Similar misinterpretations resulted in the naming of certain parts of the Moon and Mars as seas.

The case of the Piltdown Man is probably the most famous of scientific hoaxes. The problem was that much of the scientific community believed that human beings evolved from the apes and was constantly searching for the missing link - fossil evidence of bones that were half ape/half human. It proved relatively easy to fool the scientists (in 1912). They were presented with a human skull with a jaw that was apelike. The evidence was accepted, until in 1953 it was shown that the bones had been modified to make them fit together. It would be better if scientists were not always so convinced that their theories are absolutely perfect!

Unfortunately, over the years, there has been a number of instances where scientists have falsified their results in the attempt to prove a theory. Once exposed, these people have become the focus of much humiliation and shame. Indeed one scientist committed suicide as a result. The point is that most scientific observations are shared between scientists and consequently truth and honesty are very highly valued. It is important that pupils approach this topic through discussion and learn to record results and observations accurately and honestly. The idea of getting a wrong result should not be met with guilt! The meaning/interpretation of results, whilst extremely important, is secondary to the presentation of accurate ones. Poor interpretations can always be improved upon, whereas results cannot always be re-obtained. Enquiries of teachers' cheating experiences should be handled with some tact, since we should seek to avoid setting bad examples.

This topic could link with Earth in Space, evolution and possibly with some aspects of PSE.

NATIONAL CURRICULUM ASSESSMENT OPPORTUNITIES

AT17   Level 5   SofA   b

AT1   Level 4   SofA   i
       Level 5   SofA   d
AT4   Level 3
AT16   Level 4   SofA   b

EARTHQUAKES AND VOLCANOES (page 20)

Pupils are introduced to the idea of plates (as it relates to Key Stage 3) and how they affect land form and cause earthquakes and volcanoes.

BACKGROUND INFORMATION AND WAYS FORWARD

Whilst the theory of plate tectonics is called for in Level 10, there is certainly room for a simple explanation to aid understanding at the lower levels.

It was Alfred Wegener who developed the idea of continental drift. It is the understanding of this that has permitted so much else to be discovered about the world. Pangaea (all Earth) is interesting in that it helps explain why animals are so different in the different parts of the Earth. Whilst many of the continents have remained joined or have rejoined (eg the connection between North and South America), Australia was the last to break away and has remained separate ever since. Consequently, its animal life is very different from that of the rest of the world (eg its marsupials). India, once in the southern hemisphere, is still moving upwards into the Eurasian plate. The collision has formed and is forming the Himalayas! The Pacific plate is moving against the North American plate (North and South respectively), where the stress has caused the San Andreas fault.

Earthquakes occur when two plates build up great stress between them and the rock is no longer strong enough to resist. It should be understood that the resulting vibrations can have serious effects on the surface. Volcanoes are usually formed between plates, which is why they occur only in certain regions.

Pupils should enjoy manipulating cut-outs of a world map. They should first try fitting the continents together, and then cut up a tracing of Pangaea and try putting the continents in their present positions. Some effects of moving plates can be simulated by moving thin sheets of plasticine against each other.

Pupils could try to design an instrument/alarm capable of detecting sideways vibrations. They could also investigate which types of structures are least likely to collapse under such conditions. Clearly, there are links between this topic and Geography.

NATIONAL CURRICULUM ASSESSMENT OPPORTUNITIES

AT17 Level 4
     Level 5   SofA   a
     Level 6   SofA   b

AT9   Level 5   SofA   a,b
     Level 7   SofA   a
AT10 Level 5   SofA   b

THE GREENHOUSE EFFECT (page 21)

A simple account of the prime cause of the greenhouse effect is given. Pupils are asked to try and model it, and then consider the consequences.

BACKGROUND INFORMATION AND WAYS FORWARD

The Earth is still in its cycle of warming up from the last ice age. A majority of the world's scientists are now convinced that the greenhouse effect will further increase global temperatures to catastrophic levels unless checked.A basic understanding of the carbon cycle would help here. Plants are the main consumers of carbon dioxide. Consequently, fossil fuels (coal, oil) contain vast amounts of trapped atmospheric carbon dioxide. Burning them returns the gas to the atmosphere. Cutting down vegetation further increases atmospheric levels, since there are fewer plants to absorb it. The prosperous countries have long since removed the bulk of their forests and have vast amounts of space for agriculture and industry and are therefore able to maintain or increase their wealth. Many of the poorer countries are going through the same process for the same ends. The richer countries will need to offer them alternative means of wealth creation if the deforestation is to cease. Much of the energy reaching the Earth from the Sun is in the form of short wave light (ultra violet). This is able to pass through the carbon dioxide in the atmosphere. The Earth absorbs most of this, which becomes heat'. The heat is then reflected back out into space as long wave light. However, atmospheric carbon dioxide absorbs long wave light and as a result the atmosphere is warming up.

In addition to the forests, the world's greatest absorber of carbon dioxide is the oceans, which contain huge amounts of plant material (microscopic algae). Scientists are also concerned that the dumping of toxic wastes in the seas might interfere with the process here. Anything that involves burning fossil fuels will also increase atmospheric carbon dioxide levels, as will anything that results in the destruction of plants.

Of course we must have supplies of energy, but we must make every endeavour to reduce the amount that we use and waste. In simple terms, that means, for example, fewer lights and smaller cars. Generating electricity using alternative energy sources will also be part of the solution, and not just wind, wave, nuclear, hydroelectric and solar. Hydrogen gas can be burnt and the only waste produced is water! How could it be made? Would it be economic?

Increased atmospheric temperature is causing the melting of the polar ice caps. It is thought that, as a result, the sea levels are rising. This could cause the flooding of low-lying land and reduce the area on which we can live. High tides are becoming higher. Some believe that the pattern of the global climate is changing, with more storms in some places, more drought in others.

Yes, the idea of global warming was first suggested over 100 years ago. It has taken a long time to take notice because the effect has been very slow, and of course not all are agreed.

NATIONAL CURRICULUM ASSESSMENT OPPORTUNITIES

AT17	Level 4		AT9	Level 4	SofA	b
	Level 5	SofA a,b	AT13	Level 3	SofA	a,b
	Level 6	SofA a,b		Level 4	SofA	a,b,d
	Level 7	SofA a		Level 5	SofA	a,b
AT5	Level 6	SofA c		Level 6	SofA	d
	Level 7	SofA a,b				

THE CURE THAT KILLS (pages 22-23)

A description of the conditions and problems encountered in hospitals in the 19th century is given. Pupils are invited to consider these and to reflect on the contributions made by Florence Nightingale and Joseph Lister.

BACKGROUND INFORMATION AND WAYS FORWARD

This topic is self-explanatory and needs little more said here. It is somewhat 'distasteful' and in fact will stimulate the pupils' imagination.

It brings together the work of Redi, Pasteur, Nightingale and Lister and will link in with other areas such as microbiology, health and hygiene, history and PSE.

Pupils should be allowed to discuss the issues.

They could produce posters or they could make pamphlets for parents and patients. They could also be asked to design an information sheet for trainee nurses.

NATIONAL CURRICULUM ASSESSMENT OPPORTUNITIES

AT17 Level 4
      Level 6   SofA   b
      Level 7   SofA   a

AT3   Level 4   SofA   b
      Level 5   SofA   d

ACID RAIN (pages 23-24)

Pupils are asked to consider what rain would be like if it was made of vinegar. Some explanation is given of the cause of acid rain and pupils are asked to respond through a variety of tasks.

BACKGROUND INFORMATION AND WAYS FORWARD

It has been accepted for some time that this is a serious environmental problem. The main cause is the burning of fossil fuels resulting, through a series of complex reactions, in the production of sulphuric and nitric acids.

The problem, then, is created by the industrialised countries. Unfortunately, the problem is transferred to some extent into 'cleaner' countries by prevailing winds. It is generally believed that the major contributions are from coal-fired power stations but there are also other sources of this form of pollution. It is possible to reduce or stop the output of the damaging gases but it is extremely expensive and until recently governments and industry have been somewhat unwilling to invest in this area.

It is known that forests and fish livestocks are damaged, in addition to the serious erosion of buildings. What is not understood sufficiently are the likely long-term effects on the food chains.

The topic should give some relevance to pupils investigating the nature and properties of acids.

Testing smoke is an interesting exercise but teachers should appreciate that this is best done in good ventilation and preferably in a fume cupboard!

NATIONAL CURRICULUM ASSESSMENT OPPORTUNITIES

AT17	Level 4				AT5	Level 3	SofA	a
	Level 5	SofA	a			Level 5	SofA	a,c
	Level 6	SofA	b			Level 6	SofA	b
	Level 7					Level 7	SofA	a,
					AT6	Level 5	SofA	b
AT1	Level 3				AT7	Level 4	SofA	a
	Level 4					Level 6	SofA	a
	Level 5				AT8	Level 4		
	Level 6							
	Level 7							

THE NATURE OF SCIENCE

SATELLITES (page 25)

This topic explores the uses of artificial satellites, the nature of orbits and the means of keeping satellites in orbit.

BACKGROUND INFORMATION AND WAYS FORWARD

Satellites are in fact any objects in space that orbit another object, although the term is taken to mean the moons of planets. The topic concentrates on artificial satellites.

An object will continue to move in a straight line and at a constant speed providing that there is no friction or any other force acting on it. There is virtually no friction in space (more than 30 miles above the Earth's surface); however, the force of gravity is acting on a satellite. To circle or orbit the Earth, the gravitational attraction between the satellite and the Earth is used. The speed of a satellite will depend on how big its orbit is. The nearer to the Earth, the faster it needs to circle, so that it does not get pulled any closer.

A satellite can be put into a very high orbit over the Earth's equator. If the orbit is high enough, the satellite can be made to circle the Earth at the same rate that the Earth turns; so from the Earth it would seem to be stationary. Such a satellite is known as a geostationary satellite.

Artificial satellites have many uses but the main ones are to do with communications. Satellites can collect and transmit thousands of phone calls from one point of the globe to another simultaneously. They are used to photograph the regions of the Earth and to relay the information back, information such as: weather patterns, mineral deposits, likely oil locations, position of ships and aircraft for navigation, spying on enemy installations, etc. The USA is developing satellites that can destroy invading missiles (Star Wars).

Satellites are also used for making observations of outer space (free from atmospheric interference). Satellite laboratories are used for carrying out investigations in weightless conditions.

Satellites require an energy source - solar cells, batteries, fuel cells, nuclear power.

Some people are rightly anxious about the prospects of nuclear-powered satellites falling back to Earth.

NATIONAL CURRICULUM ASSESSMENT OPPORTUNITIES

AT17	Level 4			AT12	Level 6	SofA	b
					Level 7	SofA	a
AT9	Level 4	SofA	b	AT13	Level 5	SofA	b
	Level 6	SofA	c	AT16			
	Level 7	SofA	a,b				
AT10	Level 4	SofA	a,c				

INSULIN - THE LIFE SAVER (page 26)

A brief description of diabetes is given. Methods of testing for sugar are explored, and the discovery of insulin is described.

BACKGROUND INFORMATION AND WAYS FORWARD

The basic source of energy for most animals is carbohydrates. Whatever type is taken in, it must be converted into glucose which respiring cells then absorb and use.

The cells of mammals only absorb enough glucose from the blood if insulin is present in the blood. Diabetics either cannot make insulin or they make a poor quality insulin. Since cells must have energy, if they cannot take the glucose from the blood, they will get their energy from fats that are in the cells. The breakdown of fats results in the production of poisons which can induce a coma. Also, if cells cannot take sugar from the blood, then the blood sugar level will increase. If the blood sugar level is higher than normal, it will appear in the urine. So, urine containing sugar is indicative of diabetes.

Insulin is normally extracted from the pancreases of animals, though more is now being produced as a result of genetic engineering by 'safe' microbes. Many diabetics have to be given regular injections of insulin, though some can take tablets which make their pancreases work harder. The contribution made by Banting and Best was in developing the right techniques for extracting insulin from pancreases. All their research was done on dogs. (Early attempts at injecting extracts had killed animals.) Banting was awarded a Nobel prize for his discovery; he was annoyed that Best did not also get the prize so he shared the money with him.

Testing urine by taste is obviously not a very acceptable idea. Pupils will probably use Benedict's reagent or Fehlings test. A more expensive alternative is to use Clinistix, Labstix or Uristix, which are much quicker.

For fairly realistic investigations, pupils could be given suitably diluted tea with sugar added, as a urine substitute.

NATIONAL CURRICULUM ASSESSMENT OPPORTUNITIES

AT17 Level 4
    Level 5 SofA a
    Level 6 SofA a
    Level 7 SofA a

AT1 Level 3 SofA f,h,i
    Level 4 SofA f,g,h,i,j

AT3 Level 4 SofA a,b
    Level 5 SofA e
AT13 Level 4 SofA a

FRESH WATER (page 27)

Pupils are asked to decide how they would conserve a very limited supply of water (in unusual conditions). The role of water companies is briefly described and pupils are asked to consider the problem of providing pure water.

BACKGROUND INFORMATION AND WAYS FORWARD

The idea of pure water and clean rivers is very much a green issue these days.

Two thousand litres might seem a lot to the pupils. However, if they carry out a survey of the uses of water and the typical volumes involved, they should soon discover the seriousness of their predicament. Pupils will also need to carry out a data search to find out about the ways that they could purify their water.

Obviously there is a good opportunity here for the pupils to plan and carry out practical investigations. How might small amounts of water be purified in school? For example: filtering (sand and gravel in tall tubes); paper filters (would they be any good on a larger scale?); flocculation and filtering (adding small amounts of aluminium sulphate). In 1990 many people had to be compensated when they suffered mild 'poisoning' as a result of the accidental addition of too much aluminium sulphate to their local water supply. Small amounts of chlorine are often added to destroy microorganisms. Water can be mixed with activated charcoal and then filtered, or it can be passed through containers of ion-exchange resins. Pupils could distil water.

Pupils could compare water before and after passing through a small commercial water filter (obtainable from chemists and hardware stores). A survey could be made of the various types of bottled water and of the chemicals that they contain. Pupils could find out how nitrates get into water and the possible harm that they do (they may cause cancer, though there is much debate about this). They could measure pH, water hardness, residues (after evaporating) or nitrate content (test kits are available in pet fish shops).

It should be noted that many water companies add fluoride to our water. Why? Should we allow substances to be added?

There is an opportunity in this topic to investigate the water cycle.

NATIONAL CURRICULUM ASSESSMENT OPPORTUNITIES

AT17	Level 5	SofA	a,b		AT6	Level 5	SofA	b,c
						Level 6	SofA	b
AT1	Level 3				AT9	Level 5	SofA	c
	Level 4							
	Level 5							
AT5	Level 3	SofA	a					
	Level 4							
	Level 5	SofA	a,b					
	Level 6	SofA	a,b					
	Level 7	SofA	a					

KNEE DEEP IN FROGS (pages 28-29)

Pupils are given a simple introduction to the idea of natural selection (at the Key Stage 3 level). They are asked to think of reasons for the survival of some organisms and the extinction of others. Finally, pupils examine the family history of some finches and consider the effect when one is suddenly able to eat a greater range of foods.

BACKGROUND INFORMATION AND WAYS FORWARD

Whilst the theory of natural selection features at Key Stage 4, it seems appropriate to offer a simple introduction at this stage, since some understanding here relates to predator-prey relationships, food chains, variation, genetics, environment, extinction, and so on.

One of Darwin's most important observations was of the fact that each generation produces more offspring than that required simply to replace the parents. He recognised that most were eaten or died of disease before they had a chance to reproduce themselves. His most important conclusion was that the ones that did survive to reproduce must have had qualities greater than those which did not survive. Consequently, they were able to pass on these good qualities. He did not know *how* they were passed on, however, because he had no knowledge of genetics. He took the point of view that the environment (surroundings, climate, food resources, predators, etc) weeded out the weaker ones and therefore selected the strongest - natural selection!

Where do these extra qualities come from? In any population the species are not all identical; indeed there is a great deal of variation. One might expect everything to become identical by the process of natural selection but in fact new genes are always appearing and consequently new variations. This is one major reason why human beings must not interfere with the environment too much, since natural selection depends on there being a rich source of variation and natural pressures.

To a great extent, we copy natural selection in the breeding of new crops and animals. We only allow the survival of organisms with the qualities that we want (artificial selection).

In the example of the finches on page 29, note that the original parents both have the same type of beak. It is important to appreciate that the offspring with the different beak arose simply by chance and that in this example it was able to eat both seeds and insects. It was this greater choice that gave it and its offspring the greater chance of survival.

NATIONAL CURRICULUM ASSESSMENT OPPORTUNITIES

AT17	Level 4			AT4	Level 3		
	Level 5	SofA	b		Level 4		
	Level 6	SofA	b		Level 5		
	Level 7	SofA	a		Level 6	SofA	a
				AT5	Level 7	SofA	a,b
AT2	Level 3	SofA	a,b				
	Level 4	SofA	a				
	Level 6	SofA	a				

WHAT CAUSES WHAT? (page 30)

The notes below also apply to page 3 of the pupil's book. The two topics are similar in approach and the notes therefore apply equally well to both.

Pupils discuss a number of statements/hypotheses and decide whether they are reasonable or not. They then devise fair tests that will help them to discover if the idea is 'true' or not.

BACKGROUND INFORMATION AND WAYS FORWARD

The main aim is to provoke discussion and to make pupils aware that the nature of science is such that people develop ideas and then use a logical process in deciding whether these ideas are reasonable or not. The exercise will thus introduce pupils to the idea of hypotheses, although they do not need to know the actual word. The difference between good and poor science depends on the extent/rigour to which the ideas are tested. Of course not all ideas are directly testable and pupils can discover this through this topic.

People have many beliefs about the world. There is a danger that ideas can be too readily accepted without sufficient supporting evidence. Many ideas/beliefs are really myths, rather than what we might consider to be fact.

Pupils should examine the statements and decide whether they are testable or not. They should discover that to make ideas testable they may need to rephrase them. Pupils will profit by doing this exercise in small groups and much discussion/debate should be encouraged.

Some of the ideas might well be used to develop projects or explorations. However, pupils should recognise the difference between an open-ended statement and one that is stated simply and precisely enough to permit an answer of 'yes' or 'no'.

Pupils could also be made aware of 'the tentative nature of proof', ie just because a particular result is obtained, does it necessarily mean that it will always be obtained given that set of circumstances (will a coin always land head or tails)?

Once groups have produced some fair tests, they could be exchanged with those of other groups to enable further discussion/debate.

Ideally this topic is a class exercise, although it could be offered as homework. However, pupils could be asked to develop more ideas for homework, for example to make a list of superstitions and then to treat them in a similar way.

There is clearly some overlap here with aspects of Attainment Target 1 but no apology is made since pupils should discover that ideas such as these are in the very nature of science!

NATIONAL CURRICULUM ASSESSMENT OPPORTUNITIES

AT17	Level 5	SofA	a,b		AT1	Level 3	SofA	a
						Level 4	SofA	a,b,c,d

AIR POLLUTION (pages 31-32)

A brief account of industrial melanism in the peppered moth is given, together with a summary of Kettlewell's experiments with the moths in clean and air-polluted areas.

BACKGROUND INFORMATION AND WAYS FORWARD

This topic is another example of the importance of variation. It demonstrates how even a changing environment can select for or against certain characteristics of an organism.

The topic could also be used as part of an investigation into the effects of various forms of pollution. Lichens are sensitive to air pollution, especially to sulphur dioxide. In clean areas they abound on the trunks of trees, whereas in smoky industrial areas they are killed off and expose the bark to sooty deposits. The light form of the moth is very well camouflaged on the lichen-covered trees, whilst it is quite distinctive on the dark and sooty trees.

The results of Kettlewell's experiments (page 32) are clear cut. (The figures have been slightly altered to make their interpretation less complicated.) Note, however, that the answer to Question 3 should include a comment like "...it depends on whether the bark is dark or not...".

Ever since the Clean Air Act in 1956, the proportions of the dark forms have substantially reduced.

It should be possible for pupils to design a working moth trap. A successful model is likely to include some form of light.

NATIONAL CURRICULUM ASSESSMENT OPPORTUNITIES

AT17	Level 5	SofA	a,b
	Level 6	SofA	a,b
AT1	Level 3	SofA	h
	Level 4	SofA	i
	Level 5	SofA	d
AT2	Level 3	SofA	a,b,c
	Level 4	SofA	a
	Level 5	SofA	a,d
	Level 6	SofA	a

AT4	Level 4		
	Level 6	SofA	a
AT5	Level 3	SofA	a,b
	Level 5	SofA	a,c
	Level 7	SofA	a,b

NOTES